D0856476

GUEST CHECK™

Date	Table	Guests	Server	194764

APPT–SOUP/SAL–ENTREE–VEG/POT–DESSERT–BEV

The
B.T.C.
Old-Fashioned
Grocery
Cookbook

Tax

Total

NCCO 3632   GUESTCHECK™   www.nationalchecking.com   MADE IN THE USA

Guest Receipt	Amount	Guests	194764
Date			

RECIPES *and* STORIES
from a SOUTHERN REVIVAL

THE
B·T·C

OLD-FASHIONED GROCERY

COOKBOOK

ALEXE VAN BEUREN
with recipes by DIXIE GRIMES

CLARKSON POTTER / PUBLISHERS · *New York*

Copyright © 2014 by Alexe van Beuren
Photographs copyright © 2014 by Ed
Anderson

All rights reserved.

Published in the United States by Clarkson
Potter/Publishers, an imprint of the Crown
Publishing Group, a division of Random
House LLC, a Penguin Random House
Company, New York.
www.crownpublishing.com
www.clarksonpotter.com

CLARKSON POTTER is a trademark and
POTTER with colophon is a registered
trademark of Random House LLC.

The B.T.C. tomato logo design is by Coulter
Fussell and painted by Bill Warren.

Library of Congress Cataloging-in-
Publication Data
Van Beuren, Alexe.
    The B.T.C. old-fashioned grocery
cookbook / Alexe van Beuren ; with recipes
by Dixie Grimes.
        pages cm
    Includes bibliographical references and
index.
    1. Cooking, American—Southern style.
2. B.T.C. Old-Fashioned Grocery. 3. Water
Valley, Miss.—Social life and customs. I.
Grimes, Dixie. II. Title. III. Title: BTC old-
fashioned grocery cookbook.
    TX715.2.S68V35 2013
    641.5975—dc23   2013019690

ISBN 978-0-385-34500-2
eBook ISBN 978-0-385-34501-9

Printed in Hong Kong

Book design by Marysarah Quinn
Cover design by Marysarah Quinn
Cover photographs by Ed Anderson

10 9 8 7 6 5 4 3 2 1

First Edition

C·O·N·T·E·N·T·S

WHEN WE WERE FIRST APPROACHED about putting together a cookbook, Dixie and I were a little hesitant. For one thing, it seemed awfully presumptuous: We are (still) a new business, fighting for survival in our dusty small town, hauling watermelons in a station wagon, and cooking on two battered electric stoves. Plus, we're pretty busy, and carving time to write a book out of our precious spare time seemed like a daunting undertaking.

But we chose to write the book. And the big reason we were all fired up to do so wasn't necessarily the food (though Dixie's food is awesome) or the acclaim (we have no aspirations beyond making a living) but something more elemental that burns in our hearts every single day: We love Water Valley. This town has given us everything we ever wanted, and just about every day, something magical happens here. It's a special place, the likes of which do not exist just anywhere, in our country of interstates, suburbs, and chain restaurants. Granted, it's not perfect. The average income is low. I sure would like the city to repair the sidewalks and plant some trees. The school system is not nationally acclaimed. But regardless, this town provides a rich and storied life for almost every inhabitant, from the teenagers who work in the B.T.C. after school to the elderly who meet at the drugstore for early-morning coffee and Christian fellowship. This town promises to know you, through your struggles and your triumphs, and when you have passed on, it will remember you. Knowing and remembering—isn't that what we all yearn for these days?

With that in mind, we agreed to the word *revival* in the title. Let's be clear: My small grocery has not saved Water Valley. The industrial car plant down the road that employs hundreds does a lot more for folks in this town than my small store can. We have enriched Water Valley, but we have not revived it. Water Valley was here before the B.T.C., and hopefully it will be here after us (at least a century from now, as I have every intent that the B.T.C. stay open for decades upon decades).

No. The B.T.C. did not revive Water Valley. Instead, Water Valley has revived us. My family and Dixie and Cora and the other myriad souls who have opened up small businesses on Main Street are living lives that would not be possible anywhere else. Small business ownership is possible without a lot of capital, with virtually no tourism, in the kind of town where someone from the courthouse calls you to remind you to pay your taxes; the UPS man delivers your packages to where he knows you're at rather than what the address may say; and the ladies at the drugstore will gladly hold your baby if you need to, say, give a radio interview.

We live in a town of Southern revival. And every day (mostly), we give thanks.

Welcome to the B.T.C.

THERE ARE SO MANY "IFS" in this story. *If* you were to forsake the West Coast or the East Coast or Chicago or Louisiana or the coast of Maine or wherever you hailed from; *if* you were to drive to the forsaken state of Mississippi, last in so many national polls; *if* you were to detour off the beaten paths of Jackson, Ocean Springs, or Oxford; *if* you were to take the unmarked exits off of Highway 7, you would come to a little town called Water Valley.

And *if* you were to drive down the cracked main street of the three-block downtown of this small rural Deep South village, and if you were scanning the names of the storefronts, you might see my store: an old two-story brick building, biggest one in town, standing proud and true on the corner of Main Street and Wagner and boasting a sign that reads THE B.T.C. OLD-FASHIONED GROCERY, generally with a stall of Mississippi-grown red tomatoes out front.

SANDWICHES MADE TO ORDER, another sign says. And *if* you were to pull to the side of the road and come inside, you'd find a grocery store and cafe that seems wildly improbable among the dust and cotton fields of North Mississippi. Cane-sugar colas in glass bottles, local grass-fed hamburger, yellow hoop cheese with the red rind still on, handmade pastas from San Francisco, avocados priced at ninety-nine cents, artisan ice cream, warm peach fried pies on an old wooden table, and everywhere sunlight, which slants across the cracked red and blue booths in the back of the store and the copper counter in the front.

If it were lunchtime, you'd see women with pearls in their ears and men in faded shirts and work boots standing in line, waiting for salads of baby greens with goat cheese or country boy sandwiches with fat slices of bologna, dripping with mayonnaise.

You'd meet Dixie, fast-moving in a baseball cap and glasses, hands slinging sandwiches onto checked wax paper. Hard to figure she's been in the *New York Times* for her Roasted Pear and Zucchini Soup (page 48). You'd meet Alexe, fresh-faced in a red apron, busing tables and bagging groceries and asking you where you're from.

There's a good chance you'd ask Alexe how the store came to be.

You wouldn't be the first.

At this point, I'm not even sure what possessed me to open a business other than a deep and abiding vision of what *could be* in the brick building on the corner of Main Street and a certainty that no one else was going to make that vision happen. So in February 2010, I sent my husband, Kagan, an email. "Honey," it began. "Let's open a funky little produce place, with Billy Ray's milk, nothing fancy, for really cheap."

I had a two-year-old and a ten-month-old. I'd never worked a cash register. I'd never even sold anything except loaves of bread at the farmers' market I helped manage which would set up under the magnolia tree across Main Street.

Kagan thought it was a great idea.

I tried to make a business plan, but despite my expensive education, I wasn't sure how. But we did discover the results of a town study that showed Water Valley was losing nearly a half-million dollars in specialty-food sales to other towns. And besides, I wanted to sell regular food as well as the fancy stuff. I was sure we'd be an overnight success.

We agreed on a modest start-up budget, taped up black trash bags in the windows of the store, and put a big sign up front: OPENING MAY 1. We had Bill Warren, a Katrina refugee and neighbor, paint our old-fashioned-looking signs on the front of the building. We got permits and ordered dry goods and haggled with folks over used refrigerator equipment. Bought shelving from a store in Cleveland, a slicer from a country store in Tennessee, a label-printing scale off Craigslist—all the while blithely ignoring the failed businesses selling us these things.

On Saturday, May 1, 2010, the B.T.C. opened with produce thinly stretched out on the top of converted sweet potato crates and a few jars of honey and chow-chow on the shelves. We had deli meats and cheeses waiting to be sliced in the back room, but we hadn't found the time to do it and couldn't get our used label scale to work anyhow.

Folks filled the store all day long. I made countless mistakes on the cash register, like trying to sell Snooky Williams three tomatoes for $12,321.55. We sold everything we had, restocked the store, and then we waited.

And waited.

And waited.

It turned out people weren't dying to spend money with me as much as I'd thought they would be. We barely hung on that first year.

I am proud to report the B.T.C. is still here. We're a much better—and much different—store these days. I still have a million ideas and a million places to put every dollar, but the B.T.C. is holding its own, in a town of thirty-five hundred in a rural county in a depressed state.

How that came to be is a combination of a thousand different factors. But there's one that absolutely can't be ignored. Her name is Dixie Grimes.

Eighteen months into my grand vision, things had somewhat improved. I'd figured out how to use the cash register and begun a delivery program to Oxford (the nearby large and prosperous college town) that helped me make payday for my six employees. We'd been making sandwiches with sliced meats and cheeses that we stored in ice-filled sweater boxes from the dollar store. It'd become apparent that a cafe serving soups and sandwiches was something the town *and* the B.T.C. needed, but as a person with no restaurant experience already spread thin with the grocery side of the business, I didn't have the know-how or the time to make a cafe grow.

I hired five cooks in six months and learned in the process that references don't mention that someone might like to smuggle beer to work in her purse or someone else might struggle to finish a soup in less than eight hours. Trying to make a profit on soup with a huge sunk-labor cost was one of the many math, managerial, and sales lessons that I didn't know I needed.

It was a hot Saturday in September and the new cook was driving me up the wall. We had no sliced meats or cheeses in our deli cooler because the deli girl had called in sick the day before. In walked a woman in jeans with a baseball cap, a baggy T-shirt, glasses, and an ageless face. She could have been thirty; she could have been fifty. (As it turns out, she's in the middle.)

"Heard you were looking for a cook," she said.

I had people heading up front with their carts full and didn't have the time to interview anybody.

"Know how to slice?"

"Yes ma'am," she said in one of the thicker Southern accents I've heard.

"Can you start right now?"

She could. She got in the kitchen and filled my deli case up with Genoese salami and smoked turkey and Muenster cheese in record time.

On Monday, I learned her name was Dixie.

If you have trouble believing in a higher power, start a business. I'm fully convinced the Lord sent Dixie to the B.T.C. Within a month, I'd found that Dixie does the work of ten people and that she has a gift with food. Unlike me, she is a trained professional: Dixie had worked as the head chef at a wonderful restaurant on the hip square of Oxford for over ten years and had been involved with food in one way or another since she began cooking with her grandmother as a child. At some point, skill had graduated to magic.

That fall, I watched with trepidation as the cafe grew its brand-new breakfast business and lunch trade. What if Dixie left? She was highly employable with a superb reputation, and I couldn't afford to pay her what she deserved. Instead of a kitchen staff of twenty, she had her own two hands and a girl at night to do the dishes. It seemed like it would be only a matter of time before she left to work at a real restaurant.

But it turned out, as we worked around each other for month after month, that the B.T.C. was working its magic on Dixie. After so long in a high-stress restaurant environment where she didn't see her customers eat her food, she found she liked knowing her customers' names and watching their faces light up as they dug into her Curried Cauliflower Soup (page 47) or soul-raising Miss Vetra's Chicken Noodle (page 60). She liked watching Dixie's Famous Chicken Salad (page 101) fly off the shelves, and the way people moan when they talk about Breakfast Grits (page 26) and her Sausage Gravy (page 20).

These days, Dixie is firmly ensconced in a sunny old house just a few streets away from the B.T.C., and Water Valley has wrapped her up just like it did me. She has friends here. She makes my children heart-shaped sandwiches, with extra pickles on the side for Annaliese. She plans elaborate specials for holidays, like Shrimp and Grits (page 174) for Valentine's Day and Home-brined Corned Beef Brisket (page 162) for St. Patty's, just so Dr. Barry and Ramona and Mickey and all our other friends, neighbors, and customers can have something special on a special day. She fills up glass bottles with homemade salad dressings and mayonnaises and has gotten every last Yankee expatriate in our town hooked on pimento cheese.

She has made our small store sing.

We walk an odd line here at the B.T.C.

As a small business in a town of hardworking folks, we're constantly aware of cost. There's no buying asparagus for the cafe in September. Not only is it offensive to my seasonal leanings, it's just expensive. We have customers who range from folks who've never tasted fresh basil to California retirees who implore me to order crème fraîche; we sell headcheese, prosciutto, rag bologna, and feta cheese. We accept food stamps and sell artisanal gelato made with all-organic ingredients.

Our menu reflects our diverse customer base: We pay homage to Johnson's Grocery, a long-closed Water Valley institution, with our two-dollar bologna and hoop cheese sandwich; we delight the palates of our foodie customers with Dixie's inspired soups like her Wild Mushroom with Sherry Soup (page 71) and Butternut Squash with Roasted Apple Soup (page 75); and sometimes we just have fun, like when she whipped up some Tomato Caper Mayonnaise (page 124) for one day's lunch special that left everyone begging for that "funny mayonnaise" again and again.

Whether it's down-home tried-and-true or fancy, we judge everything by the same yardstick: If it's good, it stays.

Hope you enjoy.

Breakfast

CARAWAY DILL BISCUITS

SKILLET BISCUITS

SAUSAGE GRAVY

RED-EYE GRAVY

CHOCOLATE GRAVY

TOMATO GRAVY

BREAKFAST GRITS

QUICHE, THREE WAYS
ASPARAGUS *and* CRABMEAT QUICHE
WILD MUSHROOM QUICHE
ROASTED TOMATO QUICHE

BAKED EGGS *with* FRESH HERBS *and*
PARMIGIANO-REGGIANO

HONEY GOAT CHEESE FRITTATA *with*
PROSCIUTTO *and* ARUGULA

ITALIAN SAUSAGE *and* MUSHROOM
BREAKFAST CASSEROLE

BANANA BREAD

TOMATO CAPER CREAM CHEESE

SPICED HONEY CREAM CHEESE

CARAWAY DILL BISCUITS

MAKES 6 TO 8 BISCUITS

Dill is ridiculously easy to grow. And it's a pretty plant, tall and airy. I plant some every spring so that we have plenty to make Kagan's Dill Pickles (page 130). But dill is also a wonderful accent in baked goods, elevating the ordinary biscuit into something more savory. These biscuits are wonderful for that midmorning meal of brunch. Serve with thinly sliced Home-brined Corned Beef Brisket (page 162) and some good coarsely ground mustard.

2 cups all-purpose flour, plus more for rolling

1 tablespoon baking powder

1 teaspoon salt

1 tablespoon caraway seeds

1 teaspoon chopped fresh dill

¼ cup lard

½ cup whole milk

½ cup buttermilk

Preheat the oven to 400°F.

Sift together the flour, baking powder, and salt. Using a whisk, whisk in the caraway seeds and dill. Using a fork, cut the lard into the flour until you have small pea-size crumbs. Make a well in the center and pour in the milk and buttermilk. Slowly stir in the flour from the sides until the milk is evenly incorporated.

Dump the dough out onto a lightly floured work surface and knead it until smooth, about 2 minutes. Using a rolling pin that has been dusted in flour, roll out the dough until it is about ½ inch thick. Cut out biscuits with a 3-inch round biscuit cutter and put them in a cast-iron skillet with the sides touching.

Bake until the tops are golden brown, about 15 minutes.

SKILLET BISCUITS

MAKES 6 TO 8 BISCUITS

2 cups all-purpose flour, plus more
for rolling

1 tablespoon baking powder

1 teaspoon salt

¼ cup lard

½ cup whole milk

½ cup buttermilk

My love of carbohydrates started early and has stayed with me. Few things in life are so perfect as homemade biscuits straight out of the oven. I eat mine with good butter and local honey, but they're the perfect accompaniment to our gravy recipes as well.

Preheat the oven to 400°F.

Sift together the flour, baking powder, and salt. Using a fork, cut the lard into the flour mixture until you have small pea-size crumbs. Make a well in the center and pour in the milk and buttermilk. Slowly stir in the flour from the sides until the milk is evenly incorporated.

Dump the dough out onto a lightly floured work surface and knead it until smooth, about 2 minutes. Using a rolling pin that has been dusted in flour, roll out the dough until it is about ½ inch thick. Cut out biscuits with a 3-inch round biscuit cutter and put them in a cast-iron skillet with their sides touching.

Bake until the tops are golden brown, about 15 minutes.

Everybody Should Love Breakfast

THERE ARE BREAKFAST PEOPLE, and there are non-breakfast people. The Italians, for example, for all their culinary strengths, are not breakfast people. On my honeymoon in Anacapri, I had to make do with a hard roll and a slice of salami. Thankfully, it's a little different in the South.

The B.T.C.'s kitchen is simple—one person, two stoves, a couple of frying pans—and so the breakfast menu is simple, too.

Coulter Fussell—co-owner of Yalo Gallery next door, mother of two, and wife of a rock 'n' roller and lover of a good time—said once that the great thing about the B.T.C. is you can come in on a Saturday morning and grease it up with bacon, fried eggs, and biscuits topped with sausage gravy, or you can keep it light with toast and strawberries.

People don't seem to mind the limited menu. One Monday, I got to work and found a goateed fellow in a tight T-shirt and skinny jeans waiting at the door. He'd been sitting in his car for an hour waiting for us to open. He was headed home to Athens, Georgia, after recording music with Matt Patton (bassist for the Drive-By Truckers, kale lover, husband to Megan, co-owner of Yalo Gallery) and he absolutely needed to do two things: one, have biscuits and sausage gravy for breakfast again (he'd been in Sunday), and two, take a half order home to his wife.

But my favorite breakfast people of all are my Saturday folks. Water Valley is a small town that resounds with good will and cheer. Spend an hour on Main Street, just doing some errands, and you will have at least eight conversations with strangers. My father-in-law, a native Vermonter and a renowned talker, once enjoyed himself tremendously on a trip to the bank. He couldn't get over how many people he'd met. This is not a difficult place to meet folks, and we all get to know each other very well. In my own store, I can instantly identify at twenty feet anybody who has never before been in the B.T.C., and I can usually tell if they're out-of-towners to boot.

But there's a world of difference between being friendly and neighborly and actually getting friends and neighbors to spend money in your store. So when Mr. Sharp, Mr. Daum, Mr. Vaughn, and Mr. Sartain started parking their trucks behind the store and coming through the back door a full hour before we open Saturday mornings (they sit in a booth, read newspapers, drink coffee, and wait for me to take their orders), I knew our breakfast trade had turned a corner.

These men are more than my customers. Mr. Sharp gives me small business advice, and I employ his granddaughter. Mr. Vaughn's my alderman. Jerry Daum buys milk and sliced deli meats from me and talks construction methods with Kagan on a regular basis. Mr. Sartain is the owner of the hardware store down the street, a fantastic institution that's been there for forty-plus years. We talk customers and taxes and our simple business strategy of good will and impeccable service. Boy, does he set a high standard for service. One Saturday morning, I got to the B.T.C. early to start cooking and preparing for a festival later that day, only to find that the stove wouldn't cut on. I panicked and called Mr. Sartain. He sent Joey down, who within ten minutes determined that the problem wasn't the stove at all but rather that the electricity to that breaker had been cut. The hardware store's issue? No. But Mr. Sartain gave me the head of the electric department's cell phone number, and within another ten minutes the power was back on. Did any of this cost me a dime? No.

Because I don't have to take the children to school on Saturday mornings, I usually walk to work. I can't tell you how many cold mornings I've made my way down the cracked sidewalk that leads down Wagner Street to the B.T.C. and seen their trucks parked behind my store. I always smile to myself, knowing that once I step through that back door, Mr. Sartain will be holding the newspaper, Mr. Sharp will be harassing me about hash browns (which we don't sell), and the other two will be drinking coffee and smiling.

Unless, of course, it's the one Saturday a month that the Lions Club makes pancakes. In which case, all bets are off.

SAUSAGE GRAVY

1 tablespoon vegetable oil

1 pound country sausage

¼ cup all-purpose flour

3 cups heavy cream

4 dashes Tabasco sauce

1 tablespoon granulated garlic

1 tablespoon granulated onion

1 teaspoon freshly ground black
pepper

½ teaspoon dry mustard

½ teaspoon ground anise

½ teaspoon dried sage

Dash of ground cinnamon

Ground nutmeg

Salt

Skillet Biscuits (page 18)

I am what folks around here call a Yankee, though my Virginian mother's heart breaks every time she hears that. I had never tried sausage gravy before Dixie's. I still actually have never eaten anybody else's, but judging by the look on folks' faces when they eat Dixie's, it's good. Y'all should feel really special she's sharing this recipe. It came from her grandmother and is so closely guarded that we've had her cousins in the store, asking if we know how she makes it.

In a large skillet set over medium heat, heat the vegetable oil. Add the sausage and cook, breaking up any lumps with the back of a spoon, until cooked through, about 15 minutes. Stir in the flour and cook, stirring, for 7 more minutes. Using a whisk, add the cream, whisking until there are no lumps. Add the Tabasco, granulated garlic, granulated onion, pepper, mustard, anise, sage, and cinnamon. Season with nutmeg and salt to taste. Reduce the heat to low and simmer, stirring occasionally to keep the gravy from burning. When the gravy starts to thicken, after about 15 to 20 minutes, it is ready.

Serve immediately over freshly baked biscuits.

RED-EYE GRAVY

SERVES 6

4½ tablespoons unsalted butter

3 slices (¼- to ½-inch thick) good-
quality smoked country ham

¾ cup black coffee

3 tablespoons Coca-Cola (has to
be Coca-Cola)

⅛ teaspoon freshly ground black
pepper

¼ teaspoon ground cinnamon

Breakfast Grits (page 26)

The story of how we came to serve breakfast at the B.T.C. goes like this: Dixie was not yet there, and people kept asking. I figured maybe, since no one was coming into the store before lunchtime and our only competition was the gas station down the street, I should give it a shot. I hired a blonde-haired woman who spilled everything everywhere and bought an electric griddle at Target.

It was pretty much a complete disaster. Luckily, the disaster only went on for three days before Dixie came and saved us. She kept a very basic menu, added grits and sausage gravy, and limited pancakes to the weekends. These days, a whole lot of folks come though our door before noon.

Sometimes they even buy groceries.

While sausage is the only kind of gravy we serve at the B.T.C., it's by no means the only traditional gravy for a Southern breakfast. Red-eye gravy is what you get when you cook a country ham in a skillet and pour black coffee in the drippings. It is grease and caffeine and, according to Dixie, goes great with her Country Ham and Cheese Grits (page 26). You can also serve it with Skillet Biscuits (page 18).

In a cast-iron skillet set over medium heat, melt the butter. Add the ham and cook until it's golden brown on both sides, about 5 minutes total. Set the ham aside in a warm place. Add the coffee, Coke, and 4 tablespoons water to the pan, stirring with a wooden spoon and scraping the bottom of the pan to loosen any ham bits. Add the pepper and cinnamon and cook until it starts to bubble, about 7 minutes.

To serve, spoon the grits onto 6 plates, put half a slice of ham on top, and pour gravy over everything.

Chocolate GRAVY

SERVES 4

My children were born in Water Valley, so I have absolutely zero experience in child rearing anywhere else. That being said, my favorite part of having kids in a small sleepy Southern town is that they rule it. My children think that Turnage Drug Store exists so that they can climb onto its chrome-plated stools and order ice cream; they believe that D&D's House of BBQ is there solely to dispense their favorite dish of baked beans and pulled pork with absolutely no sauce; they adore going to church because the preacher gives them lollipops and sends them down to "children's church" where they color pictures and play games; they beg to accompany Kagan to Sartain's True Value hardware store so they can pretend to be dogs in the plastic dog houses out on the sidewalk. Fall is for soccer, spring is for T-ball, summer is for multiple blazing-hot birthday parties with plastic baby pools and elaborate sprinklers. (Why did we all have summertime babies? In Mississippi?)

This town lets children be children. Children, in fact, are the whole reason for chocolate gravy. It caters to the fiendish sweet tooth inside every child and, according to Dixie, is mostly reserved for a weekend treat.

¼ cup **Dutch cocoa powder**

¼ cup **sugar**

¼ cup **all-purpose flour**

½ teaspoon **ground cinnamon**

⅛ teaspoon **salt**

2 cups **heavy cream**

¼ cup (½ stick) **unsalted butter**

1 tablespoon **Coca-Cola (has to be Coca-Cola)**

Skillet Biscuits (page 18)

In a bowl, whisk together the cocoa powder, sugar, flour, cinnamon, and salt.

In a medium saucepan set over medium heat, combine the cream, butter, and Coke. Heat the mixture, stirring constantly, until it just starts to boil (you're looking for small bubbles), about 10 minutes. Whisk in the cocoa mixture a little at a time, and then cook, whisking constantly, until the gravy starts to thicken, about 10 minutes.

Serve immediately over freshly baked biscuits.

TOMATO GRAVY

Southerners firmly believe that little in life can't be improved by a ripe tomato. Preferably homegrown and sun-ripened. For those who steer clear of sweet things first thing in the morning and aim more toward savory, tomato gravy on top of biscuits is a perfect way to wake up.

2 tablespoons bacon grease

2 tablespoons all-purpose flour

2 cups plain tomato juice

½ cup tomato puree

⅛ teaspoon Worcestershire sauce

Dash of Tabasco sauce

⅛ teaspoon sugar

⅛ teaspoon dry mustard

⅛ teaspoon freshly ground black pepper

Dash of ground cloves

Salt

Skillet Biscuits (page 18)

In a large cast-iron skillet set over medium heat, heat the bacon grease. Stir in the flour to make a roux and cook, stirring constantly, until the flour is cooked through and begins to brown, about 7 minutes. Gradually whisk in the tomato juice until smooth. Add the tomato puree, Worcestershire sauce, Tabasco, sugar, mustard, pepper, and cloves. Season with salt to taste. Cook until the gravy thickens, about 20 minutes.

Serve over freshly baked biscuits.

BREAKFAST GRITS

4 cups heavy cream

1 cup (2 sticks) unsalted butter

2 cups fresh stone-ground grits

Salt

Between 8:00 AM and 10:30 AM Monday through Saturday, the odds are good someone will be sitting in a back booth eating grits. People love our grits so much we put a bowl of 'em on the menu, and it comes with a side of sausage or bacon for $3.99.

People from the North think of grits as a peculiar obsession of those who hail below the Mason-Dixon Line. That is because they have never had good grits. Good grits start with the grits itself. Ours come from our friend and neighbor Becky Tatum, who lives one block over from me and whose custom milling business, Delta Grind, provides fine restaurants all around the area with her top-of-the-line stone-ground grits and meal. Becky drops off her wares weekly, usually as a barter trade (groceries for grits—what's not to love?), so they're always fresh.

Dixie cooks them the way they need to be cooked—with whipping cream and butter. They are absolutely not heart healthful. They are absolutely delicious. Work out a balance, but for heaven's sake, don't make a low-fat version. That's how grits get a bad reputation.

In a large saucepan set over high heat, bring 6 cups of water, the cream, and the butter to a medium simmer. Gradually whisk in the grits. Reduce the heat to low and cook, stirring constantly, until creamy and thick, about 1 hour. Salt to taste and serve immediately.

Variations

BAKED GRITS CASSEROLE: A grits casserole sounds bizarre, but the fact of the matter is you may end up cooking the casserole more than plain old grits. What's the big difference? The casserole is a richer and thicker concoction and a delicious foundation on which to serve anything you desire. Follow the directions for the Three-Cheese Grits. Let cool for 20 minutes. Meanwhile, preheat the oven to 425°F and spray a 9 × 13-inch casserole dish with nonstick cooking spray. Fold 4 beaten eggs into the grits and scoop the mixture into the prepared casserole dish. Bake until golden brown, 30 to 45 minutes.

The grits casserole will keep in the freezer for up to 3 months. For best results, freeze it before baking; thaw overnight in the refrigerator, and then bake according to the recipe.

DIXIE'S TOMATO GRITS: Follow the cooking directions at left, and then add two 10-ounce cans of mild Ro-Tel tomatoes and their juices.

THREE-CHEESE GRITS: Follow the cooking directions at left, and then whisk in 1 tablespoon chopped garlic (use the garlic in a jar, which is mellower than raw) and 2 cups each shredded extra-sharp Cheddar cheese, pepper jack cheese, and smoked Gouda.

DIXIE'S JALAPEÑO CHEESE GRITS: Follow the directions for the Three-Cheese Grits, and then add 1½ cups chopped jalapeños.

DIXIE'S COUNTRY HAM AND CHEESE GRITS: Follow the directions for the Three-Cheese Grits. While the grits are cooking, melt 2 tablespoons butter in a cast-iron skillet set over medium heat. Brown both sides of a slab of country ham that's about ¼ inch thick in the butter, about 5 minutes on each side. Take the ham out of the skillet and drain it on paper towels. Chop the ham and add it to the cheese grits. Serve with Red-Eye Gravy (page 22).

QUICHE, *Three Ways*

I am absolutely wild about quiche, but there are two obstacles that keep me from serving it. Y'all, Water Valley, Mississippi, is a wonderful town and I love it with almost every fiber of my soul. But I think folks are so scarred from cold, rubbery quiches sitting in glass cases in overpriced gourmet marketplaces that a tiny warning bell goes off in their minds if I even mention it. Not to mention we're already making them exotic soups, sell quinoa, have dry-cured olives in our new deli case, and last week Dixie made watermelon salad with feta, red onion, mint, and balsamic reduction. I think we need to stagger our gastronomic introductions. We'll do quiche eventually, though.

These here are completely awesome quiches. Serve with a salad and glass of wine for a light supper, or make them ahead for a weekend brunch. Just don't serve them cold, for heaven's sake.

ASPARAGUS *and* CRABMEAT *quiche*

SERVES 4 TO 6

1 teaspoon extra-virgin olive oil

1 teaspoon unsalted butter

8 large asparagus spears, trimmed

1 garlic clove, chopped

Salt and freshly ground black pepper

¼ cup dry white wine

Juice of ½ lemon

5 egg yolks

1½ cups heavy cream

Dash of ground nutmeg

1 (9-inch) store-bought pie shell, baked (see Note, opposite)

½ pound Fontina cheese, shredded (1½ cups)

6 to 8 ounces (1 cup) jumbo lump crabmeat, shells and cartilage discarded

Preheat the oven to 425°F.

In a sauté pan set over medium to medium-high heat, heat the oil and butter until bubbly but not smoking. Add the asparagus and toss until coated. Add the garlic and season with salt and pepper. Cook until the asparagus is bright green and just tender, about 6 minutes. Pour in the wine and lemon juice, and set aside.

In a medium bowl, whisk the egg yolks until light and fluffy, and then whisk in the cream and nutmeg.

Reduce the oven temperature to 400°F. Arrange the asparagus spears in the pie shell in a star pattern with the tips pointing toward the outside. Sprinkle in half of the cheese, followed by all of the crabmeat, and then top with the remaining cheese. Pour the egg mixture into the shell.

Bake until golden brown on top and set in the center, or until a toothpick inserted in the center comes out clean, 1 hour and 15 minutes. Let cool for 30 minutes before slicing. Serve warm.

WILD MUSHROOM *quiche*

Preheat the oven to 325°F.

In a sauté pan set over medium heat, heat the butter. Add the mushrooms, leeks, garlic, thyme, rosemary, salt, and pepper. Cook until the mushrooms are soft, about 10 minutes. Add the sherry and cook, stirring, until it has evaporated, about 5 minutes. Drain the mushrooms, discarding any liquid, and set aside.

In a medium bowl, whisk the egg yolks until light and fluffy, and then whisk in the cream and nutmeg.

Put half of the mushroom mixture in a single layer in the bottom of the pie shell and sprinkle with half of the cheese; repeat the layers. Pour the egg mixture into the shell.

Bake until golden brown on top and set in the center, or until a toothpick inserted in the center comes out clean, 1 hour and 15 minutes. Let stand for 30 minutes before slicing. Serve at room temperature.

Note

For a homemade pie crust, use the crust recipe in Fried Pies (page 202). Half of the dough is enough for a 9-inch pie. Roll the dough out, transfer it to a 9-inch pie dish, and crimp the edges. Line the crust with parchment paper and fill it with dry beans. Bake for 20 minutes at 425°F. Remove the paper and beans, lower the oven temperature to 375°F, and bake (keep an eye on it) until golden brown, 15 more minutes. Remove from the oven and let cool before making the quiche.

- ¼ cup (½ stick) unsalted butter
- 1 cup sliced button mushrooms
- 1 cup sliced chanterelle mushrooms
- 1 cup sliced shiitake mushrooms
- ½ cup sliced leeks
- 1 garlic clove, chopped
- ¼ teaspoon chopped fresh thyme
- ¼ teaspoon chopped fresh rosemary
- ⅛ teaspoon salt
- ⅛ teaspoon freshly ground black pepper
- ⅛ cup sherry (Dixie prefers Harveys Bristol Cream)
- 5 egg yolks
- 1½ cups heavy cream
- Dash of ground nutmeg
- ¼ pound Gruyère cheese, shredded (1 cup)
- 1 (9-inch) store-bought pie crust, baked (see Note)

ROASTED TOMATO *quiche*

10 to 12 ¼-inch-thick tomato slices (use homegrown or vine ripened)

Extra-virgin olive oil

⅛ teaspoon dried basil

⅛ teaspoon dried oregano

Salt and freshly ground black pepper

5 egg yolks

1½ cups heavy cream

1 (9-inch) store-bought pie shell, baked (see Note, page 29)

¼ pound provolone cheese, shredded (1 cup)

1 cup grated Parmigiano-Reggiano cheese

SERVES 4 TO 6

Preheat the oven to 425°F.

Spread the tomato slices on a baking sheet in a single layer, not overlapping. Drizzle with enough oil to coat them and sprinkle with the basil, oregano, and salt and pepper. Roast for 15 to 20 minutes, until the tomatoes start to shrink. Let cool for 30 minutes.

In a medium bowl, whisk the egg yolks until light and fluffy, and then whisk in the cream.

Arrange half of the roasted tomato slices in a single layer (there should be a little bit of room in between slices) in the bottom of the pie shell. Sprinkle half of both cheeses on top; repeat the layers. Pour the egg mixture into the shell.

Bake until golden brown on top and set in the center, or until a toothpick inserted in the center comes out clean, 1 hour and 15 minutes. Let sit for 30 minutes before slicing. Serve warm.

BAKED EGGS
with Fresh Herbs and Parmigiano-Reggiano

½ cup panko bread crumbs

½ cup grated Parmigiano-Reggiano
cheese

3 garlic cloves, chopped
(1 tablespoon)

1 teaspoon chopped fresh tarragon

1 teaspoon chopped fresh thyme

1 teaspoon chopped fresh chives

4 large eggs

¼ cup heavy cream

2 teaspoons unsalted butter

2 tablespoons dry vermouth

Salt and freshly ground black
pepper

2 heirloom tomatoes, sliced for
serving

½ cup Hellmann's mayonnaise, for
serving

Sliced ciabatta bread, toasted, for
serving

SERVES 2

As someone who's spent her entire life cooking, first in her grandmother's kitchen and then as her livelihood (Dixie has cooked for a living more than two decades), Dixie doesn't tend to go home after work and fire up the stove again. But Sundays are different. Sundays are the days when she has a pile of booty from the Saturday farmers' market, which sets up downtown under the magnolia tree, and she's rested—and anyhow, it's *Sunday*. (Dixie does not work on the weekends. It's not a religious thing. It's Dixie. Folks have begged her, but ain't no way, no how, that she will fry you an egg on Sunday. Monday through Friday, folks.)

In Mississippi, Sundays are family days. Many stores and restaurants are closed; streets tend to be deserted between 9:00 AM and noon, since everyone's in church; and just about everybody I know spends their afternoons hanging out at the matriarch's house waiting on supper—or out at the lake catching supper.

Back when Dixie was dating a nurse named Lela, they would host brunch at their house on Sundays. Tired of having eggs scrambled or fried, Dixie wanted to try something different. She came up with this way of baking them in a rich and creamy sauce, composed in little individual baking dishes that make for a beautiful presentation.

Preheat the broiler.

In a medium bowl, combine the bread crumbs, cheese, garlic, tarragon, thyme, and chives.

In 2 separate bowls, crack 2 eggs into each bowl, being careful not to break the yolks.

In a small saucepan set over low heat, combine the cream, butter, and vermouth. Heat, stirring, until lightly simmering, 5 to 6 minutes. Turn off the heat, but leave the pan on the stove.

Put 2 small to medium gratin dishes on a baking sheet. Put them under the broiler for 2 minutes to heat them up. Take them out of the oven and divide the cream mixture between them. Gently pour the eggs into the gratin dishes, and sprinkle with salt, pepper, and a generous amount of the bread crumb mixture. Broil for 7 to 8 minutes, until the eggs are set, or a little less if you want your eggs runny.

Serve hot with the tomatoes, mayonnaise, and toast on the side.

HONEY GOAT CHEESE FRITTATA
with Prosciutto and Arugula

SERVES 6 TO 8

Inside Dixie's very Southern heart, there's a corner reserved for Italy. She loves and adores all things Italian, from buffalo mozzarella to good olive oil to basically all cured meats.

This frittata pays homage to Italy with the sweet twist of honey goat cheese. A staple of our deli counter, honey goat cheese has a pleasantly mellow taste that tempers the sharpness inherent in all chèvre.

8 large eggs

1 teaspoon chopped fresh chives

⅛ teaspoon kosher salt

½ teaspoon freshly ground black pepper

½ teaspoon unsalted butter

½ teaspoon extra-virgin olive oil

½ cup chopped prosciutto (3 ounces)

½ cup arugula

½ cup crumbled honey goat cheese

Preheat the broiler.

In a medium bowl, whisk together the eggs, chives, salt, and pepper.

Heat a 12-inch oven-safe skillet over medium heat until it's hot but not smoking. Add the butter and oil, give the skillet a swirl, and then add the prosciutto. Cook, stirring, for 1 minute, and then add the arugula and cook until it is wilted, 2 to 3 minutes. Pour the egg mixture into the pan, and using a heat-resistant rubber spatula, lift up the sides of the eggs, letting any uncooked eggs run underneath. As soon as the eggs start to set on the bottom, remove the pan from the heat. Dot the top of the frittata with the crumbled goat cheese.

Put the skillet in the oven and broil until lightly browned and fluffy, about 4 minutes. Remove from the oven, let sit for 5 minutes before cutting, and serve.

Everybody Always Asks: B.T.C.?

SO, IT WAS WINTER OF 2010. The idea for the store was drifting just below the surface, percolating gently, trying to get my attention, and I kept shoving it down. It'd cost money. Zero experience. I had an infant and a toddler. I'd never really succeeded at anything besides school and keeping house, and a store, a store was just such a . . . large idea. So much bigger than a table with some tomatoes.

Out of the blue, my mother called me.

"You'll never believe what I found," she told me. (She'd been cleaning out her desk, apparently, an event in itself.)

She proceeded to read me a list I made when I was about seven years old. In my shaky block handwriting, I'd written:

> "When I grow up, I'd like to be
> 1. A writer.
> 2. An actress.
> 3. A merchant, who shall be fair and just to all, and not charge too much but have fair prices, and live well but not too well and not take really expensive vacations or anything like that."

(My mother, incidentally, had no idea that I was hatching such a crazy scheme as a grocery store at the time.)

I hung up the phone, looked at the ceiling, and said, "Fine."

The name of the store comes from the quote that kept haunting my nights and dreams as I pondered opening the store. It's from Gandhi, and it goes like this: You must be the change you wish to see in the world. A powerful call to action, and so I named my store the B.T.C., with *old-fashioned* thrown in because Mickey Howley said no one would know what my store was like from three initials.

To tell the truth, I had no idea anyone would ever ask me about the store's initials. I mean, what does A&W stand for (root beer), or A&P (supermarket)? I have no idea.

People ask me every day, y'all. And every time, I feel deeply embarrassed as I explain to all and sundry Mississippians that my store is named after a quote from Gandhi. But if someone asks, I always tell the truth.

I am trying to be the change I'd like to see in the world. It's a difficult process.

It'd be nice to say I have never regretted the decision to open the store. Let me tell you: crouching in the back of a vehicle in a Mississippi summer, moving watermelons that weigh more than my four-year-old—for an hour? Staring at my Excel spreadsheet with a stack of invoices next to me? Getting to work by seven o'clock in the morning every Saturday? Sure. Sometimes it crosses my mind that maybe I could have just kept driving a half hour to get my damn milk.

But in my bones, I know it was meant to be. I was born to be a small-town grocer; Dixie was fated to walk through the door in my hour of need; and the B.T.C. had to exist in Water Valley—it could never achieve the magic it has in any other building on any other street in any other town.

ITALIAN SAUSAGE *and* MUSHROOM *Breakfast Casserole*

½ pound sweet Italian sausage, casings removed

1 small fennel bulb, chopped (½ cup)

1 cup sliced white mushrooms

8 eggs

2 cups heavy cream

1 teaspoon dry vermouth

½ teaspoon chopped fresh oregano

½ teaspoon ground nutmeg

½ teaspoon kosher salt

½ teaspoon freshly ground black pepper

12 slices white bread, crusts removed, cubed

2 cups grated sharp white Cheddar cheese

SERVES 8

Reasons to make a breakfast casserole: Your in-laws are in town, and you need to spend the early morning vacuuming. High school boys are spending the night, and it's better to serve them something contained rather than getting roped into standing next to the stove for a solid hour making pancakes to order. Someone needs sustenance in the way of food and the whole neighborhood knows it, which means the recipients of largesse might have eighteen lasagnas and nothing for breakfast.

This particular casserole is savory enough for dinner, but the eggs make it breakfasty. Teenage-boy approved.

Grease the bottom and sides of a 9 × 13-inch baking dish with butter.

In a skillet set over medium heat, cook the sausage, breaking it up with the back of a wooden spoon, until browned throughout, 10 to 12 minutes. Using a slotted spoon, transfer the sausage to a paper-towel-lined plate to drain. Discard all but 1½ tablespoons of the grease in the pan. Add the fennel and mushrooms and cook, stirring, until the fennel is soft, 10 minutes. Remove the pan from the heat.

In a medium bowl, whisk together the eggs, cream, vermouth, oregano, nutmeg, salt, and pepper. In the bottom of the prepared baking dish, spread half of the bread, and top with half of the cooked sausage, half of the fennel mixture, and half of the grated cheese; repeat the layers with the remaining ingredients. Cover with plastic wrap and refrigerate overnight.

The next day, preheat the oven to 350°F. Remove the plastic from the dish and bake until the casserole is golden brown and a toothpick inserted in the center comes out clean, 45 minutes. Let sit for 10 minutes before serving.

BANANA BREAD

As a grocer, I have to admire the ubiquity of bananas. This tropical fruit grows absolutely nowhere in North America, but out of all the fruits the B.T.C. stocks, it is the one I absolutely cannot run out of without deeply offending my customers.

This means that at times I show up in the kitchen with an apron full of bananas too ripe to sell. Happily for me, the B.T.C. wastes very little, and so Cora turns those fine fruits into moist and delicious loaves of banana bread that are so good folks harass us when we're out. They are a special favorite of our Thursday lunch old-men crowd, who like to buy one and split it eleven ways, in true Water Valley patriarch fashion.

3 cups all-purpose flour

1 teaspoon baking powder

1 teaspoon baking soda

1 teaspoon ground cinnamon

Dash of salt

2 large eggs

1½ cups sugar

1 cup vegetable oil

¾ cup sour cream

1 teaspoon vanilla extract

4 very ripe bananas, mashed

1 cup chopped pecans (optional)

Preheat the oven to 350°F. Grease four 8-inch loaf pans with butter.

In a small bowl, combine the flour, baking powder, baking soda, cinnamon, and salt.

In a medium bowl, beat the eggs. Add the sugar, oil, sour cream, and vanilla. Add the bananas and pecans (if using) and stir well. Add the flour mixture a little at a time, stirring until all of it is incorporated. Pour the batter into the prepared loaf pans.

Bake until golden brown on top and a toothpick inserted in the center comes out clean, about 30 minutes. Remove the pans from the oven and let cool in the pans for about 10 minutes. Turn the loaves out onto wire racks and cool completely.

TOMATO CAPER CREAM CHEESE

1 (8-ounce) package Philadelphia cream cheese, room temperature

¼ cup capers, drained

½ tomato, cored and chopped (¼ cup)

1 teaspoon finely chopped red onion

⅛ teaspoon chopped fresh dill

1 teaspoon granulated garlic

My husband is an amazing man who has opened my eyes to many possibilities in life. Really. I know it's kind of fashionable to bash your spouse in public, but I really got a good one, much to my own surprise. I didn't know husbands could come in *awesome* edition.

This relates to cream cheese in this way: He makes sandwiches with it. I never heard of such a thing. Cream cheese is for bagels! And that is the *law*!

Turns out those sandwiches are pretty good.

When we make pinwheel trays for tailgating events down here in Mississippi, we cut wraps into little circles about three-quarters of an inch wide and fan 'em out so they look like pinwheels. Dixie makes them with this cream cheese, pit-roasted ham, and Muenster cheese; and the cream cheese holds the wrap together and doesn't ooze and leak and soggify the way mayonnaise would.

It'd be good on a sandwich, too. Or a bagel.

In a food processor, blend the cream cheese, capers, tomatoes, onion, dill, and granulated garlic until well incorporated.

The cream cheese will keep in an airtight container in the refrigerator for 7 days.

SPICED HONEY CREAM CHEESE

MAKES 1 CUP

We live in the land of biscuits instead of bagels. On a trip back to Virginia, I met up with my aunt and uncle at a Charlottesville institution called Bodo's Bagels, where excellent—and low-cost—bagels are served up daily. Annaliese and Caspian got cinnamon raisin with butter and adored them. A couple days after the visit, back home in Mississippi, Annaliese asked if we could have really good round things with holes in them again. (Between that and her amazement at the delicacy that is steak over dinner the other night, I sometimes wonder who exactly I am raising my children to be.)

The only ways bagels could be better is if they had this cream cheese on them. Creamy and interesting, it dresses up any breakfast. Also makes a fantastic garnish for sweet soups such as Butternut Squash with Roasted Apple Soup (page 75) or Roasted Pumpkin Soup (page 72).

1 (8-ounce) package Philadelphia cream cheese, room temperature

¼ cup honey

1 teaspoon ground cinnamon

1 teaspoon ground allspice

½ teaspoon ground cloves

In a food processor, blend the cream cheese, honey, cinnamon, allspice, and cloves until well incorporated.

The cream cheese will keep in an airtight container in the refrigerator for 7 days.

Soups for Every Season

WINTER

CHICKEN STOCK (*and* BOILED CHICKEN)

SPINACH ARTICHOKE BISQUE

CURRIED CAULIFLOWER SOUP

ROASTED PEAR *and* ZUCCHINI SOUP

WHITE BEAN CHICKEN CHILI

LOADED BAKED POTATO SOUP

SPRING

MISSISSIPPI CATFISH GUMBO

CHICKEN GUMBO

MISS VETRA'S CHICKEN NOODLE

SUMMER

SHRIMP *and* SWEET CORN CHOWDER

VEGETABLE BEEF SOUP *with* BUTTER BEANS

SUMMER SQUASH SOUP

DOWN-HOME TOMATO SOUP

FALL (AKA FOOTBALL)

WILD MUSHROOM SOUP *with* SHERRY

ROASTED PUMPKIN SOUP

BUTTERNUT SQUASH SOUP *with* ROASTED APPLE

HOTTY TODDY BEER CHILI

Out of all the places I've ever lived, Mississippi has the mildest winters. And the most bitterly resented. We cheerfully cope with frigid temperatures for three months: December, January, and February. But one year, when March 1 turned out to be bone-chilling cold with light flurries, you would have thought that Christmas had been canceled. People often plant tomato seedlings in January around here, and if they can't get in the garden to at least set out some kind of seedlings by the middle of March, there will be a few grumpy green-fingered folks complaining in a big way.

On days that are so foul you'd think folks would rather stay at their desks or in their offices than venture out, Dixie fills the stockpot to its brim. The uglier the day, the more people will hustle up to the kitchen door and completely bypass the rest of the menu to order a big bowl of soup, making sure it comes with corn bread, and where's the tea, thank you, ma'am. They sit and move their spoons like they are taking communion, in earnest silence until the center of them thaws. And then they begin to talk again, all the while the spoon flashing, until the sides of the bowl are scraped clean.

It's not uncommon for customers to beckon me over and put in a to-go order for supper or for their wife or their mama or their children that night.

CHICKEN STOCK
(and Boiled Chicken)

MAKES 2 QUARTS

Before we dive into Dixie's soups, y'all should learn to make stock. Store-bought will work just fine and there's no shame in it, but if you have a stringy old hen running around your backyard or see a manager's special at the grocery store, this is a good use for it. A fabulous foundation for these soups, good homemade stock also comes in handy for making risotto, rice, quinoa, or cooking vegetables country-style.

And there's a bonus: The cooked chicken meat can be used in lots of other recipes, like Dixie's Famous Chicken Salad (page 101), Chicken Pot Pie with Parsnips and Roasted Leeks (page 149), and Chicken Spaghetti (page 147).

1 (5-pound) hen

1 large yellow onion, quartered

2 medium carrots, cut in half

2 celery stalks, cut in half

1 lemon, cut in half

2 garlic cloves

10 sprigs fresh parsley

10 sprigs fresh thyme

1 tablespoon kosher salt

8 whole black peppercorns

Put the chicken, onion, carrots, celery, lemon, garlic, parsley, thyme, salt, and peppercorns in an 8- to 10-quart stockpot. Cover with water, bring to a simmer, and cook, uncovered, for 4 hours.

Remove the chicken and set it aside to cool. Strain the stock through a colander into a bowl and discard the solids. Pour the stock into a container and refrigerate overnight.

Pick the chicken meat off the bones, cleaning off any scum from cooking as you go. Use immediately, refrigerate for up to 2 days, or freeze for up to 2 months.

SPINACH ARTICHOKE *Bisque*

SERVES 8

½ cup (1 stick) unsalted butter

2 tablespoons extra-virgin olive oil

1 medium yellow onion, finely chopped

1 large fennel bulb, finely chopped (1 cup)

Dash of crushed red pepper flakes

¼ cup dry white wine

¼ cup Pernod, plus more for serving

8 cups Chicken Stock, homemade (page 45) or store-bought

2 pounds fresh spinach

2 cups diced artichoke hearts, thawed if frozen or drained if jarred in water

1 teaspoon Worcestershire sauce

4 cups heavy cream

⅛ teaspoon white pepper

⅛ teaspoon ground nutmeg

Salt

6 to 8 ounces (1 cup) jumbo lump crabmeat, shells and cartilage discarded, for serving

Sometimes I think the best meals are the ones your bones are craving. You know what I'm talking about? When every cell in your body aches for a certain combination of flavors and vitamins? One day a few years ago, when I was about four months gone, as they say down here, with Caspian, I was exhausted. Maybe it was because I was expecting, maybe it was because Annaliese was not yet a year old and had slept basically two combined hours since birth. Who knows. Anyhow, I needed nourishment in a big way, and Kagan made a great dinner: steak, creamed spinach, a navel orange, and a bowl of mint chocolate-chip ice cream for dessert. The iron and the folates and the vitamin C and the sugar sank into my bloodstream and I fell asleep early. Slept all night, for the first time that year, until seven o'clock in the morning. I awoke feeling like I could, after all, live another day.

This soup is like a pourable version of creamed spinach. For days when you need something wonderfully decadent and chock-full of vitamins at the same time, make this bisque.

In an 8-quart stockpot set over medium-high heat, heat the butter and oil. Add the onion and fennel and cook, stirring, until the vegetables are translucent, about 10 minutes. Add the pepper flakes and white wine and cook, stirring, until it comes to a simmer, about 15 minutes. Add the Pernod and cook off the alcohol, about 5 minutes. Add the stock, spinach, artichoke hearts, and Worcestershire sauce and cook until the spinach has wilted, about 15 minutes. Add the cream, white pepper, and nutmeg. Turn the heat to low, and simmer gently for 30 minutes. Season with salt to taste.

To serve, ladle the soup into serving bowls, drizzle with Pernod, and sprinkle 2 tablespoons of jumbo lump crabmeat on top. The soup can be stored in an airtight container in the refrigerator for 4 days.

CURRIED
Cauliflower Soup

SERVES 6 TO 8

The odds are high that if you come to Water Valley, you'll meet Mickey Howley. He is a tall man with a shiny head who wears odd T-shirts and talks like he came from deepest Jersey, which is apparently how old-school, true-blue New Orleans natives sound. He's lived in Turkey, worked on a shrimp boat, got a master's degree in creative writing, operated his own trucking business, taught high school, and worked as a Mercedes mechanic. Mickey and his wife, Annette, co-run Bozarts Art Gallery, and he serves as our town's Main Street manager, which means he has a finger in every pie in town.

He's also my buddy—and one tight-fisted, hard-to-please son of a gun. When Dixie first made this cauliflower soup, Mickey put down his spoon and announced that it was a killer. That it was extraordinary.

Unprecedented praise, folks.

Dixie serves this with coconut milk and a spoonful of mango chutney drizzled on top.

2 tablespoons extra-virgin olive oil

1 medium yellow onion, finely chopped

2 tablespoons minced shallots

2 tablespoons minced peeled fresh ginger

2 garlic cloves, minced

½ cup dry white wine

1 large head cauliflower, chopped (12 cups)

8 cups Chicken Stock, homemade (page 45) or store-bought

1 cup coconut milk

2 tablespoons fresh lime juice

2 tablespoons honey

1 tablespoon Sriracha chili sauce

2 tablespoons ground turmeric

2 tablespoons curry powder

1 tablespoon granulated garlic

1 tablespoon onion powder

1 teaspoon white pepper

1 teaspoon ground ginger

1 teaspoon ground fennel

1 teaspoon ground anise

⅛ teaspoon ground cinnamon

Pinch of saffron (optional)

2 cups heavy cream

Salt

In an 8-quart stockpot set over medium to medium-high heat, heat the oil. Add the onion, shallots, and fresh ginger and cook until soft, 5 to 7 minutes. Add the garlic and cook for 5 more minutes. Stir in the white wine, scraping up any brown bits stuck on the bottom of the pan. Add the cauliflower and toss to coat. Add the stock, coconut milk, and lime juice. Cook until the cauliflower is soft, about 15 minutes.

Remove the pan from the heat, and using an immersion blender or working in batches with a regular blender, puree until smooth. Return the pan to the heat and bring the soup back up to a simmer. Add the honey, Sriracha, turmeric, curry powder, granulated garlic, onion powder, pepper, ginger, fennel, anise, cinnamon, and saffron (if using). Cook for 30 minutes, until it comes to a simmer. Add the cream and simmer for 15 minutes (do not let it boil). Salt to taste.

Serve hot. The soup can be stored in an airtight container in the refrigerator for 7 days.

Roasted Pear and
ZUCCHINI SOUP

8 ripe yet firm Bosc pears, peeled, cored, and cut into 1-inch slices

6 tablespoons extra-virgin olive oil

1 medium Vidalia onion, chopped

2 shallots, chopped

1 garlic clove, minced

6 to 7 medium zucchini, diced (8 cups)

2 tablespoons Pernod

8 cups Chicken Stock, homemade (page 45) or store-bought, or vegetable stock

2 cups apple juice

1 tablespoon honey

2 cups fresh spinach

¼ cup pear or apple butter

Juice of 1 lemon

1 teaspoon Worcestershire sauce

1 teaspoon ground anise or ground fennel

1 teaspoon granulated garlic

1 teaspoon granulated onion

½ teaspoon dry mustard

½ teaspoon ground cinnamon

⅛ teaspoon ground allspice

⅛ teaspoon ground ginger

⅛ teaspoon white pepper

SERVES 6 TO 8

This is the B.T.C.'s most celebrated soup, mostly because it's the most esoteric and was featured in the *New York Times*. It's also really, really good. There's a lady in Oxford who has us make it when she's having a dinner party and she passes it off as her own. We're all right with that, as long as she pays her $8.99/quart.

As exotic as it sounds, this soup also reminds Dixie powerfully of her maternal grandmother, Miss Vetra, who raised Dixie in a little white house on University Avenue in Oxford. Miss Vetra (pronounced "Vee-tra," with a male twin named Vettra, pronounced "Vet-tra," and there's a great story behind that) was a hardworking lady who'd clerked in the mayor's office for decades. She and her husband scrimped and saved to own that house free and clear, and they didn't have a lot of extra money to spare. But Miss Vetra, who was a painter and an artist in the kitchen, loved food—everything from chicken and dumplings and sausage gravy to fancy things. Starting when Dixie was very young, she made a habit of taking Dixie to all the fine restaurants within driving distance. The one rule was that Dixie had to try something she'd never had before.

Miss Vetra also had a pear tree in her yard that she adored.

Decades later, Dixie makes this soup partially in memory of her grandmother and the pear tree. It's the soup Miss Vetra would have wanted to try.

Preheat the oven to 425°F.

Spray a baking sheet with nonstick cooking spray. Toss the pears in 4 tablespoons of the oil and spread them out flat on the baking sheet. Roast until caramelized, about 20 minutes. Set aside to let cool.

In an 8-quart stockpot set over medium heat, heat the remaining 2 tablespoons oil. Add the pears, onions, and shallots and cook, stirring, until soft, about 10 minutes. Add the garlic and cook for 5 more minutes. Add the zucchini and cook until soft, about 15 minutes. Add the Pernod and stir, scraping up any brown bits on the bottom of the pan, 2 to 3 minutes. Add the stock and apple juice and bring to a simmer. Add the honey, spinach, pear butter, lemon juice, Worcestershire sauce, anise, granulated garlic, granulated onion, mustard, cinnamon, allspice, ginger, and white pepper. Simmer for 1 hour.

Remove the pan from the heat, and using an immersion blender or working in batches with a regular blender, puree until smooth. Add the cream and bring the soup back to a low simmer. Season with salt and pepper to taste. Remove the pot from the heat and whisk in the cold butter.

Serve hot. The soup can be stored in an airtight container in the refrigerator for 7 days.

4 cups heavy cream

Salt and freshly ground black pepper

½ cup (1 stick) unsalted butter, cold and cut into pieces

WHITE BEAN CHICKEN CHILI

SERVES 8

¼ cup extra-virgin olive oil

1 medium Vidalia onion, finely chopped

1 small green bell pepper, cored, seeded, and finely chopped (½ cup)

Freshly ground black pepper

2 garlic cloves, minced

⅛ cup tequila (Dixie likes Jose Cuervo)

1½ cups fresh, frozen, or canned corn kernels (if fresh, from about 4 cobs)

2 (10-ounce) cans mild Ro-Tel tomatoes

1 (7.4-ounce) can diced mild green chiles

2 (14.5-ounce) cans cannellini beans, rinsed and drained

2 (14.5-ounce) cans great northern beans, rinsed and drained

8 Dixie's Grilled Chicken Breasts (recipe follows), finely chopped

12 cups Chicken Stock, homemade (page 45) or store-bought

Juice of 2 limes

1 tablespoon Worcestershire sauce

6 to 8 dashes Tabasco sauce

1½ teaspoons cornmeal

2 bay leaves

2 tablespoons ground cumin

1 tablespoon chili powder

People in this town have been known to stand in front of the menu board and talk about soup.

"Vegetable beef, that's my favorite," someone will say.

"Really? That's mighty fine but I sure do love the . . ." someone else will say.

Kagan's a fool for the Hotty Toddy Beer Chili (page 76). I am a surprised and fervent fan of the Roasted Pumpkin Soup (page 72). Miss Debbie at the farm-supply store buys up the Loaded Baked Potato Soup (page 52). But without a doubt, one of the top three most popular soups is the White Bean Chicken Chili. Everybody likes it: the rock stars, the professionals, the old men, the young women. The ladies at the bank, the teachers, the folks from the hospital. Great as a weekday supper and substantial enough for a Super Bowl party.

This soup freezes beautifully and pairs well with Negra Modelo.

In an 8-quart stockpot set over medium heat, heat the oil. Add the onion, bell pepper, and a pinch of black pepper. Cook until the vegetables are soft, about 10 minutes. Add the garlic and cook for 5 more minutes. Remove the pot from the heat and add the tequila. Return the pot to the heat and cook until the tequila has evaporated, 5 minutes. Add the corn, tomatoes, chiles, cannellini beans, and great northern beans. Stir well, and then add the grilled chicken, stock, lime juice, Worcestershire sauce, Tabasco, cornmeal, bay leaves, cumin, chili powder, coriander, white pepper, paprika, and mustard, and season with salt and black pepper to taste. Bring to a low simmer and let cook, uncovered, for 1 hour and 30 minutes, stirring occasionally to keep the beans from burning.

Remove the bay leaves. Scoop out 2 cups of the soup, puree it in a food processor, and stir it back in the pot. Cook for 15 minutes.

Divide the soup among 8 bowls. Serve with bowls of the crushed tortilla chips, cheese, sour cream, olives, avocado, lime wedges, and cilantro for folks to put on top as they please.

1/8 teaspoon ground coriander

1/8 teaspoon white pepper

1/8 teaspoon sweet paprika

1/8 teaspoon dry mustard

Salt

Optional toppings

4 cups crushed tortilla chips

3/4 pound pepper jack or Cheddar
cheese, shredded (2 cups)

1/2 cup sour cream

1/4 cup chopped black olives

4 avocados, pitted and sliced

8 lime wedges

Leaves from 1 bunch fresh cilantro

DIXIE'S GRILLED CHICKEN BREASTS

SERVES 8

In a large glass bowl, whisk together the oil, soy sauce, sherry, honey, lime juice, granulated garlic, and pepper flakes (if using). Season with salt and pepper. Add the chicken and toss well. Spread the chicken in a single layer in a glass baking dish and cover with the marinade. Cover the dish with plastic wrap and refrigerate for 2 to 4 hours.

Take the chicken out of the refrigerator 30 minutes before cooking.

Heat a grill to medium to medium-high heat.

Brush the grill grates with a little vegetable oil so that the chicken won't stick. Grill the chicken for 5 to 6 minutes per side. The chicken is done when the internal temperature is 170°F. Transfer the chicken to a plate and let rest for 10 minutes before serving.

Store in an airtight container in the refrigerator for up to 3 days.

1/4 cup extra-virgin olive oil

1/2 cup regular or dark soy sauce

2 tablespoons sherry (Dixie likes
Harveys Bristol Cream)

1 tablespoon honey

Juice of 1 lime

1 teaspoon granulated garlic

1/8 teaspoon crushed red pepper
flakes (optional)

Salt and freshly ground black
pepper

8 (6- to 8-ounce) boneless,
skinless chicken breasts,
trimmed

LOADED BAKED POTATO SOUP

SERVES 8

¼ cup extra-virgin olive oil

6 strips thick-cut apple-wood smoked bacon, chopped

1 medium Vidalia onion, finely chopped

1 large shallot, finely chopped

1 small fennel bulb, finely chopped (½ cup)

1 garlic clove, minced

½ cup dry vermouth

6 medium to large Yukon gold potatoes, peeled and chopped

12 cups Chicken Stock, homemade (page 45) or store-bought

4 dashes Tabasco sauce

1 tablespoon granulated onion

1 tablespoon granulated garlic

½ teaspoon dried basil

½ teaspoon white pepper

⅛ teaspoon sweet paprika

1 cup sour cream

4 cups heavy cream

¼ pound extra-sharp Cheddar cheese, shredded (1 cup)

1 cup grated Parmesan cheese

½ cup (1 stick) unsalted butter, cold

Salt

Once upon a time, Dixie did not work at the B.T.C., and other "cooks" did. I have many stories about these short-tenured cooks. One such tale comes to mind every time Dixie makes potato soup. I had hired a hippie who refused to shave his beard stubble, so the health department required him to wear a beard net as he cooked and made sandwiches to order. He was also swarthy, smelly, and slow. I could deal with the hippie earth aspect (hey, I have hippie credentials myself!), but when he took *eight hours* to make potato soup one day, we parted ways, which was probably best for both our karmas.

This soup does not take eight hours to make. It is also the best potato soup I've ever tasted: thick, creamy, and deliciously rich.

In an 8-quart stockpot set over medium heat, heat the oil. Add the bacon and cook until crisp, about 10 minutes. Transfer the bacon to a paper-towel-lined plate to drain.

Add the onion, shallot, and fennel to the pot and cook, stirring, until soft and translucent, about 10 minutes. Add the garlic and cook for 1 minute. Add the vermouth and cook, stirring and scraping any up any browned bits on the bottom of the pan, until evaporated, about 5 minutes. Add the potatoes, stir well, reduce the heat to low, and cook for 5 minutes. Add the stock and cook until the potatoes are just soft, about 15 minutes.

Remove the pot from the heat. Using an immersion blender, or working in batches with a regular blender, blend until the mixture is smooth. Put the pot back over medium heat and bring the soup to a simmer. Add the reserved cooked bacon, Tabasco, granulated onion, granulated garlic, basil, pepper, and paprika. Bring to a simmer and cook until lightly bubbling, 10 to 15 minutes. Whisk in the sour cream until blended, and then add the heavy cream. Bring the soup back up to a simmer, but do not boil. Whisk in both

cheeses a little at a time until they are completely incorporated. Remove the pot from heat, whisk in the butter, and season with salt to taste.

Ladle the soup into bowls and serve with the toppings on the side (if desired).

Optional toppings

¾ pound Cheddar cheese, shredded (2 cups)

½ cup sour cream

4 strips cooked bacon (about ¼ cup)

½ cup finely chopped fresh chives

S·P·R·I·N·G

Spring is everybody's favorite time of year, is it not? Every fall, I try to plant a few bulbs in strategic locations—out in front of the kitchen window, down in the garden, in random patterns in the middle of the lawn—because I know my eyes will be hungry for the sight of daffodils as wintertime winds down.

I love daffodils and have become mildly obsessed with them since moving to Mississippi, where there are loads of these beautiful flowers in every shape and size. There are your classic yellow trumpets, and five-petaled ones that look like stars with coquettish, rose-colored pistils in their middles. There are tiny yellow ones, smaller than a buttercup, that smell intensely of jonquil. There are crazy yellow and green waterfall-like blossoms that the old-timers call scrambled eggs. I once took a picture of every different kind of daffodil I saw and made a photo album to show my mom. I found eighteen within a half mile of my house.

The determination of these bulbs and the facts of the town's history are linked in my mind. Water Valley has weathered some tough times, and all throughout the town there are bare lots with old concrete steps leading to nowhere, some with the original family's name etched at the base of the steps. The only thing left on these lots? Daffodils.

For many decades, Water Valley was a prosperous Mississippi town. It was the county seat, with plenty of area farmers to come in and shop on Saturdays, and the center of the ICCR railroad, which had its maintenance hub here. Even after the railroad left town in the 1950s, Water Valley was hopping until a decade of unrelated events happened.

First, beginning before World War II and until the early 1950s, nearly 40 percent of the county's premier farmland was annexed by the Corps of Engineers, which constructed Enid Lake to control the Mississippi River's flooding. The bypass was completed by 1973, which meant that every car passing through the state north to south no longer had to drive through downtown. There followed the opening of Wal-Mart in the early 1980s in Oxford, coupled with the slackening of the 1970s record gas prices. And then, in 1984, the coup de grâce: a severe tornado that leveled many homes, killed seven people, and took out several handsome nineteenth-century buildings on Main Street and most of the Baptist church.

My opinion—and granted, it's my opinion—is that things were heading south for Main Street merchants in between all those events. The ones that could stayed open—like Sartain's Hardware, which has been open for more than forty years, and Turnage Drug Store, open since 1905. But there wasn't much economic incentive for folks to rebuild from the devastation or invest money in downtown at all. (Two very notable exceptions: Mechanics Bank and Cornerstone Rehabilitation, God bless 'em, both of which retrofitted old buildings on Main Street in the 1990s to serve as their businesses' headquarters.)

To be frank, there still really isn't a lot going on here. The population of Water Valley (thirty-five hundred) hasn't changed for decades and people these days conduct a lot more business elsewhere than they used to. But despite the very real economic problems in this small town, springtime in Water Valley always comes again. There's a sense of hope: New people have moved here, businesses have opened, buildings are being renovated, houses are being bought and sold. The tone of the town has changed, too. We're not even close to harvest season yet, but like early spring, there's a sense of good things a-comin'.

MISSISSIPPI CATFISH GUMBO

SERVES 8

My taste buds aren't as brave as some people's, so I've always been leery of gumbo. I just can't handle spice. Kagan and I once went to India for three weeks and spent the whole time eating toasted white bread with the consistency of Styrofoam. Embarrassing, but true. We tried, y'all, but neither one of us can handle hot sauce, jalapeños, strong curries, or most gumbos.

But Dixie made her catfish gumbo as a special one day and said we had to try it. And though it's legit enough to please the Cajuns in our crowd, I loved it, too. The pop of the okra seeds, the zing of the vinegar, the shreds of flaky catfish throughout—it's perfect, even for milder palates like mine. (If you are one of those who like everything very spicy, dial up the Tabasco sauce).

"We need to put this on the permanent menu," I said.

Dixie started laughing, bent over, shook her head from side to side.

And then she said yes.

Dixie recommends using catfish from Pride of the Pond, though any Mississppi-farmed catfish will do.

Preheat the oven to 375°F.

Pat the catfish fillets dry with a paper towel, and then lightly coat both sides in the Blackening Seasoning. Spray a baking sheet with nonstick cooking spray and arrange the fillets on the sheet. Bake until flaky, 30 minutes. Set aside to let cool.

In an 8-quart stockpot set over medium heat, heat the oil. Add the onion, bell pepper, and celery and cook, stirring, until soft, about 10 minutes. Add the garlic and cook for 5 more minutes. While stirring constantly, add the flour and cook until golden brown, about 7 minutes. Whisk in the stock, Coke, white wine, coffee, and tomato paste. Whisk until smooth, and bring to a low simmer, about 15 minutes. Add the okra, tomatoes, lemon juice, Kitchen Bouquet, vinegar, Worcestershire sauce, Tabasco, bay leaves, and thyme. Bring to a simmer and cook for 15 minutes. Add the Old

(recipe and ingredients continue)

6 to 8 catfish fillets
(each 5 to 7 ounces)

2 tablespoons Blackening
Seasoning (recipe follows)

¼ cup extra-virgin olive oil

1 medium onion, finely chopped

1 yellow bell pepper, cored,
seeded, and chopped

4 celery hearts, chopped

1 clove garlic, minced

¼ cup all-purpose flour

8 cups seafood stock or Chicken
Stock, homemade (page 45)
or store-bought

1 can Coca-Cola (has to be
Coca-Cola)

¼ cup dry white wine

2 tablespoons black coffee

1 (6-ounce) can tomato paste

½ to ¾ pound fresh okra, chopped
(4 cups), or 1 (10-ounce)
package frozen, thawed

2 (10-ounce) cans mild Ro-Tel
tomatoes

Juice of 1 lemon

1 tablespoon Kitchen Bouquet
sauce (see Note, page 56)

1 tablespoon balsamic vinegar

1 tablespoon Worcestershire sauce

6 to 8 dashes Tabasco sauce

2 bay leaves

⅛ teaspoon chopped fresh thyme

1 tablespoon Old Bay seasoning

1 tablespoon granulated garlic

1 tablespoon onion powder

⅛ teaspoon freshly ground black
    pepper

Salt

Perfect White Rice (page 200)

2 tablespoons filé powder, plus
    extra for garnish (see Note;
    optional)

Notes

*Kitchen Bouquet is a browning and
seasoning sauce, which you can find
in your grocery's spice aisle.*

*Filé powder is a seasoning made
from dried and ground sassafras
leaves. It's a traditional ingredient
in gumbos, but if you can't find it, it's
okay to leave it out.*

Bay, granulated garlic, onion powder, pepper, and salt. Reduce the
heat to low and cook for 1 hour and 15 minutes, until thickened.

Crumble the cooked catfish into the pot, breaking it up into small
to medium pieces. Add the filé powder (if using) and cook for
45 more minutes on a low simmer. Remove the bay leaves. Season
with salt to taste.

Serve in bowls, topped with rice and sprinkled with a little filé
powder (if using).

BLACKENING SEASONING

1 cup sweet paprika

¼ cup granulated onion

¼ cup granulated garlic

2 tablespoons salt

2 tablespoons white pepper

2 tablespoons cayenne pepper

2 tablespoons dry mustard

1 teaspoon dried thyme

MAKES ABOUT 1¾ CUPS

In a large bowl, whisk together the paprika, granulated onion,
granulated garlic, salt, white pepper, cayenne, mustard, and
thyme until all lumps are gone. Store in a Mason jar in a cool,
dark place for up to 6 months.

CHICKEN GUMBO

SERVES 6 TO 8

2 tablespoons extra-virgin olive oil

2 tablespoons finely chopped
smoked ham

2 strips thick-cut apple-wood
smoked bacon, chopped
(2 tablespoons)

1 medium onion, finely chopped

6 celery hearts, finely chopped
(1 cup)

1 small green bell pepper, cored,
seeded, and chopped (1 cup)

2 small carrots, finely chopped
(½ cup)

2 garlic cloves, minced

½ cup dry white wine

2 (14.5-ounce) cans diced fire-
roasted tomatoes

6 cups Chicken Stock, homemade
(page 45) or store-bought

2 tablespoons Worcestershire
sauce

2 tablespoons ketchup

1 tablespoon balsamic vinegar

1 tablespoon Tabasco sauce

1 teaspoon Kitchen Bouquet sauce
(see Note, page 56)

2 teaspoons chopped fresh
rosemary

2 teaspoons chopped fresh thyme

6 Dixie's Grilled Chicken Breasts
(page 51), chopped

½ pound fresh okra, chopped
(1½ cups), or 1 (10-ounce)
package, frozen, thawed

In Mississippi, catfish is as common a delicacy as pastrami is in New York City. But I remember when I lived in places where when people referred to tea, they meant the steaming beverage; where *meat-and-three* held no meaning for me; where I had barely heard of catfish, let alone knew it as a grocery store staple.

If you live somewhere like that, maybe chicken gumbo would be the gumbo recipe for you. It is traditional, it is delicious, and there will be no wild-eyed haunting of the grocery store frozen seafood department. Serve in bowls, topped with the rice and chopped onions, sprinkled with a little filé powder.

In an 8-quart stockpot set over medium heat, heat the oil. Add the ham and bacon and cook until the bacon fat is rendered, about 10 minutes. Add the onion, celery, bell pepper, and carrots and cook, stirring, until soft, 10 minutes. Add the garlic and cook for 5 more minutes. Add the wine, stirring and scraping up any browned bits on the bottom of the pot. Add the tomatoes, stock, Worcestershire sauce, ketchup, vinegar, Tabasco, Kitchen Bouquet, rosemary, and thyme. Bring to a simmer and add the chicken, okra, bay leaves, filé powder (if using), onion powder, oregano, sage, black pepper, and cayenne. Reduce the heat to low and simmer, stirring occasionally, for 1½ hours, or until it reaches the desired thickness. Remove the bay leaves. Season with salt to taste.

Serve in bowls, topped with rice and the green onions.

4 bay leaves

2 teaspoons filé powder (see Note, page 56; optional)

1 teaspoon onion powder

1 teaspoon dried oregano

1 teaspoon dried sage

1 teaspoon freshly ground black pepper

⅛ teaspoon cayenne pepper

Salt

Perfect White Rice (page 198)

½ bunch green onions, chopped

MISS VETRA'S CHICKEN NOODLE

SERVES 8

6 tablespoons extra-virgin olive oil

1 large onion, finely chopped

6 celery hearts, finely chopped
(1 cup)

1 cup chopped mushrooms

2 medium carrots, finely chopped
(1 cup)

1 garlic clove, minced

1 (4-ounce) jar chopped pimientos

½ cup dry white wine

2 quarts Chicken Stock, homemade
(page 45) or store-bought

Juice of 1 lemon

2 tablespoons granulated onion

2 tablespoons granulated garlic

1 teaspoon freshly ground black
pepper

Meat from 1 Boiled Chicken
(page 45)

2 tablespoons chopped fresh
parsley

2 tablespoons chopped fresh
thyme

2 tablespoons chopped fresh
rosemary

2 tablespoons chopped fresh
tarragon

1 (16-ounce) package egg noodles

Salt

Decades ago, Miss Vetra made this chicken noodle soup for Dixie whenever she showed the slightest signs of being sick, and Dixie swears it always cured what ailed her. Now Dixie makes it for us. It is not jazzed up. It is not fancy. It is the homemade version of what comes out of a Campbell's soup can, without the BPA or sodium worries, which, if you're like me, is a big enticement. I ate a lotta Campbell's soup as a kid and I remain fond of it, but these days, when my children are snuffling, cracking open a can seems like the irresponsible option and I count myself fortunate that I have this savory, ever so slightly spicy chicken noodle soup instead.

We use noodles handmade at Eduardo's Pasta Factory in San Francisco, but any high-quality noodles will work, as long as they're not overly thin (this is not the place for angel hair). Dixie also recommends egg noodles. Employ as needed for spring colds.

In a 12-quart saucepan set over medium-high heat, heat the oil. Add the onion, celery, mushrooms, and carrots and cook, stirring, until soft, about 10 minutes. Add the garlic and pimientos and cook for 5 more minutes. Add the white wine and stir, scraping up any browned bits on the bottom of the pot. Add the stock, lemon juice, granulated onion, granulated garlic, and pepper. Bring to a simmer, add the chicken, reduce the heat to low, and cook for 1 hour.

Add the parsley, thyme, rosemary, tarragon, and noodles. Cook until it starts to simmer, about 30 more minutes. Season with salt to taste and serve.

S·U·M·M·E·R

Kagan and I moved to Mississippi in October 2006. We waltzed into two months of bright clear blue skies, no humidity, with chilly crisp nights and daytime highs of about sixty-five degrees. It was magnificent. As we drove past fields with great trees arched against the perfect skies, shopped in businesses where personal checks were encouraged, and ate fried catfish for the first time, we wondered why in the world everybody didn't live in Mississippi.

All these years later, I still don't know the answer. But I suspect the summers of thick, sticky humidity, oppressive sun, and inevitable drought might have something to do with it.

So picture this: a summer day, say, in July, when everyone who can be is on vacation and Main Street is parched and dry. Dogs lie panting under porches. The brave flowerpots the Garden Club ladies have set out are visibly radiating heat. The only thing anyone ever wants to buy is a tomato, because the entire town's eating tomato sandwiches for supper; it's too hot to turn on the oven.

And still Dixie, in the kitchen of the B.T.C., makes soup. Hot soups. Because people still walk through our front door, exhale in thanks for the air-conditioning, and order a big bowl for lunch, day in and day out.

1 cup Old Bay seasoning

1 pound shrimp

1 cup vegetable oil

1 medium onion, chopped

6 celery hearts, chopped (1 cup)

2 medium carrots, chopped (1 cup)

1 garlic clove, minced

1 small green bell pepper, cored, seeded, and chopped

1 cup all-purpose flour

½ cup dry vermouth

8 cups seafood stock or Chicken Stock, homemade (page 45) or store-bought

4 cups fresh or frozen corn kernels (if fresh, from about 10 cobs)

1 tablespoon Worcestershire sauce

4 dashes Tabasco sauce

2 bay leaves

2 tablespoons chopped fresh thyme

2 teaspoons chopped fresh rosemary

½ teaspoon white pepper

SHRIMP *and* SWEET CORN CHOWDER

SERVES 4 TO 6

Middle-aged and handsome, Eddie Rogers is a born-and-bred Water Valley boy. We met when I was running our town's farmers' market and got irrationally excited at the sight of the five-gallon bucket full of egg-size red plums sitting in the back of his truck. In the world's thickest drawl, he said that he had got to sell these, but if I wanted, I could come out to his place tomorrow and pick up my own bucket, which he'd have ready and waiting. I asked him how much. He considered. Then he said, "Ten dollars," with a calculating look.

All these years later, Eddie is still one of my favorites. Lately, he's been leaving me five-gallon buckets full of small, bright green okra at the back door of the B.T.C., free of charge, because (in his words) he is proud of my store and wants us to do well.

Eddie also happens to be the area's foremost farmer of sweet corn. Baxter Jones specializes in watermelons, and Kenny Harmon does peas, but Eddie does corn.

If you are lucky enough to find some sweet corn and some fresh shrimp at the same moment in time, you can't go wrong with this chowder. It is outrageously good. I said this with such conviction the last time Dixie made it that a Catholic priest bought a couple quarts without ever tasting it.

Bring 6 cups of water and Old Bay to a boil in a 4-quart stockpot set over high heat. Add the shrimp and cook until they start to curl and turn pink, 3 minutes. Using a mesh strainer, transfer the shrimp to a bowl of ice water. Let sit for 2 minutes, drain the shrimp, and put them on paper towels to dry. Peel, devein, and chop the shrimp.

In an 8-quart stockpot set over medium heat, heat the oil. Add the onion, celery, carrots, garlic, and bell pepper and cook, stirring, until the vegetables are just soft, about 15 minutes. Stir in the flour and cook until it begins to turn golden brown, about 7 minutes.

Whisk in the vermouth and stock until the flour is incorporated and there are no lumps. Add the fresh or frozen corn, Worcestershire sauce, Tabasco, bay leaves, thyme, rosemary, and pepper. Bring to a low simmer and cook for 1 hour.

Reduce the heat to low and add the shrimp, cream-style corn, and cream. Cook, stirring occasionally, for 30 more minutes. Remove the bay leaves. Season with salt to taste. Remove the pot from the heat and stir in the butter until incorporated.

Serve in bowls, topped with the crumbled bacon.

2 (16-ounce) packages frozen cream-style corn, thawed (4 cups; Dixie prefers frozen but canned will work)

4 cups heavy cream

Salt

1 cup (2 sticks) unsalted butter, cold and cut into cubes

4 strips cooked bacon, crumbled

VEGETABLE BEEF SOUP *with Butter Beans*

SERVES 8 TO 10

Think about your town, your city, your suburb. Where do you buy your food?

The odds are good you shop weekly at a Wal-Mart, a Kroger in the South or a Hannaford's in the North, a Trader Joe's or a Whole Foods in Austin, San Francisco, or Portland. Maybe you live in some place with a thriving farmers' market or a wonderful bakery or an indispensable specialty market, and you prefer those places. I don't know. But in general, Americans typically drive to big stores with a lot in them, stock up for the week, and then drive home.

Water Valley is like that. We have a family-run Piggly Wiggly supermarket that has serviced Water Valley for over fifty years, and many people shop there. Others make weekly or so trips to stock up at the Wal-Mart and Kroger twenty miles north. Some even go to Sam's in Southaven, a full hour away. But no one exclusively shops at the B.T.C. We are always an extra stop for people, and sometimes, in this world of convenience and limited time, that's a hard sell.

In this small town exists a group of about ten elderly men. (They are going to give me merry hell when they read this. But y'all, every single hair on every one of your heads is g-r-a-y.) Their wives do the grocery shopping and have done so for decades; some of those wives shop with us and some of them don't.

But when we opened the cafe inside the store, these men began to come to lunch with us once a week. At first, they squeezed into two separate booths and pulled up metal folding chairs. I went to Memphis at some point and bought them a big round table that can comfortably seat all of them from a diner getting torn down for a new CVS.

They show up every Thursday, and I can't tell you how this has comforted me on days when I wasn't sure our store would make it. They come in and joke with me and place difficult orders and halve sandwiches and make a ridiculous mess with napkins and chip bags. And I am thankful.

All this goes to say that at least once a month, on a Thursday morning, Dixie makes her vegetable beef soup with butter beans, because it's the old men's favorite. It's my favorite, too. An unlikely thing for a yuppie Virginia girl and a bunch of male Mississippian elders to have in common, but there

(recipe continues)

2 tablespoons extra-virgin olive oil

1 medium onion, finely chopped

2 celery hearts, finely chopped

3 medium carrots, chopped (1½ cups)

1 small orange bell pepper, cored, seeded, and finely chopped

1 cup sliced mushrooms

3 pounds ground chuck

2 (14.5-ounce) cans diced fire-roasted tomatoes

1 garlic clove, chopped

12 cups beef stock

2 tablespoons Worcestershire sauce

6 tablespoons tomato paste

1 large bay leaf

1 cup fresh Silver Queen corn (from about 4 cobs)

1 cup fresh or frozen baby lima beans

1 cup fresh or frozen purple hull peas

1 cup fresh or frozen green peas

1 cup chopped fresh string beans

3 small yellow squash, chopped (2 cups)

1 tablespoon granulated onion

1 tablespoon dried basil

1 teaspoon freshly ground black pepper

Salt

Dixie's Corn Bread (page 197)

you go. While we do make it year-round, it's best in the summer when all the vegetables are in season. This is a big batch of soup, so if you have extra, it freezes beautifully.

In a 12-quart stockpot set over medium heat, heat the oil. Add the onion, celery, carrots, bell pepper, and mushrooms. Cook, stirring, until the onions start to become translucent, about 10 minutes. Add the chuck a little at a time, stirring well, and cook until browned through, about 15 minutes. Add the tomatoes and garlic and cook, stirring, for 5 minutes. Add 6 cups of water, the stock, Worcestershire sauce, tomato paste, and bay leaf. Bring to a simmer and cook for about 10 minutes. Add the corn, lima beans, purple hull peas, green peas, string beans, squash, granulated onion, basil, and pepper. Season with salt to taste. Reduce the heat to low and let simmer for 2 hours, until the soup is thick. Remove the bay leaf.

Serve in bowls with corn bread.

SUMMER SQUASH SOUP

SERVES 6 TO 8

Squash soup sounds weird but it is fantastic. It manages to be slightly sweet, thick, and rich yet light at the same time. A pretty yellow bisque, it sells out every time we serve it. One soul among four will order it, and the other three ask for a taste. The skeptics then order some too and ask for more to take home for supper. We always use local squash because I generally have too many people trying to sell me too much of it in July.

In an 8-quart stockpot set over medium heat, heat the butter and oil. Add the squash, onion, bell pepper, shallot, and garlic and cook, stirring, until the squash is soft, about 15 minutes. Add the wine and cook until it has evaporated, 5 minutes. Add the stock, Worcestershire sauce, Tabasco, basil, granulated garlic, granulated onion, anise, sugar, turmeric, white pepper, and pepper flakes. Bring the mixture to a simmer and cook for 30 minutes.

Remove the pot from the heat, and using an immersion blender or working in batches with a regular blender, puree until smooth. Return the pot to low heat and add the cream and nutmeg. Bring to a simmer and cook for 30 more minutes, until slightly thick. Season with salt to taste.

In a medium bowl, make a slurry (see Note) by combining the cornstarch and a ½ cup of cold water until smooth. Whisk the slurry into the simmering soup. Cook for 10 minutes, or until the soup is as thick as you like.

Serve the soup in bowls, drizzled with a little cream and sprinkled with nutmeg.

Note: *A slurry is a mixture that helps thicken soups and sauces in a lighter fashion than would a roux. Add it to a soup that's lightly simmering, because it won't work if the soup is not bubbling. Whisk well to incorporate it, and it should thicken the soup instantly. The longer the soup is on the heat, the more it'll thicken.*

½ cup (1 stick) unsalted butter

2 tablespoons extra-virgin olive oil

3 pounds yellow squash, chopped

1 large Vidalia onion, chopped (1½ cups)

½ small yellow bell pepper, cored, seeded, and chopped (¼ cup)

1 medium shallot, chopped (2 tablespoons)

2 garlic cloves, minced

¼ cup dry white wine

8 cups Chicken Stock, homemade (page 45) or store-bought

1 teaspoon Worcestershire sauce

Dash of Tabasco sauce

1 teaspoon dried basil

1 tablespoon granulated garlic

1 tablespoon granulated onion

1 teaspoon ground anise

⅛ teaspoon sugar

⅛ teaspoon ground turmeric

⅛ teaspoon white pepper

Dash of crushed red pepper flakes

4 cups heavy cream, plus more for serving

⅛ teaspoon ground nutmeg, plus more for serving

Salt

½ cup cornstarch

DOWN-HOME TOMATO SOUP

SERVES 6 TO 8

½ cup (1 stick) unsalted butter

1 tablespoon extra-virgin olive oil, plus more for serving

3 pounds fresh tomatoes, cored and chopped, or 2 (28-ounce) cans chopped tomatoes, drained

1 medium onion, chopped (1 cup)

2 medium carrots, chopped (1 cup)

1 small fennel bulb, chopped (½ cup)

2 tablespoons finely chopped red bell pepper

2 tablespoons finely chopped celery hearts

1 shallot, chopped

2 garlic cloves, chopped

1 bay leaf

¼ cup dry white wine

2 tablespoons Pernod

8 cups Chicken Stock, homemade (page 45) or store-bought

1 tablespoon Worcestershire sauce

1 tablespoon red wine vinegar

3 dashes Tabasco sauce

1 teaspoon chopped fresh thyme

1 teaspoon chopped fresh rosemary

1 teaspoon chopped fresh parsley

1 teaspoon chopped fresh tarragon

1 teaspoon chopped fresh basil

About the first of May, folks start calling the store and dropping by. They are black, white, young, old, Baptist, Methodist, AME, single, married, rich, poor, and middling, but they all have the same thing on their mind: homegrown tomatoes.

Now nobody calls them "local." *Locavore, locally sourced, carbon footprint*—none of these buzz words have reached our neck of the woods. The concepts these trendy terms are trying to reconnect us with have never gone away in Mississippi, especially when it comes to tomatoes. The area farmers never set tomato plants out until after Easter, so there are no homegrown tomatoes to be had before June 1 at the earliest. But that doesn't stop everybody from harassing me for what I think of as Mississippi's household icon.

Our first year, it seemed like all I could sell folks was one single tomato. A store full of fresh produce and pasta from Eduardo's in San Francisco and wheels of cheese and freshly roasted coffee and bread baked that morning and glass-bottled Brown Dairy milk and all I could sell people was what? One. Single. Tomato.

This tomato soup is not your typical mild-tempered or easygoing comfort food. Dixie calls it down home, mostly because she uses the cracked and splitting tomatoes farmers sell us for cheap after thunderstorms, but I'd call it kick-ass. It's got a zing. Unlike many tomato soups, Dixie's uses no cream and little butter. Instead, she's found a way to make a different kind of tomato soup, one that manages to be healthy and delicious.

Oh. I'd like to point out one more thing: the store's logo, which we came up with two years into the B.T.C.?

One tomato.

In an 8-quart stockpot set over medium heat, heat the butter and oil. Add the tomatoes, onion, carrots, fennel, bell pepper, celery, shallot, garlic, and bay leaf. Cook, stirring, until the tomatoes soften and start to break down, 20 minutes. Add the wine and cook until it has evaporated, about 5 minutes. Add the Pernod and cook until it has evaporated, about 5 minutes. Add the stock, Worcestershire sauce, vinegar, Tabasco, thyme, rosemary, parsley, tarragon, basil, sugar, mustard, paprika, and pepper. Bring the mixture to a simmer, reduce the heat to low, and cook for 1 hour. Remove the bay leaf.

Season with salt to taste. Remove the pot from the heat, and using an immersion blender or working in batches with a regular blender, puree until smooth.

To serve, ladle the soup into bowls, drizzle with oil, sprinkle with the cheese, and top with the croutons.

⅛ teaspoon sugar

⅛ teaspoon dry mustard

⅛ teaspoon sweet paprika

⅛ teaspoon freshly ground black pepper

Salt

3 tablespoons grated Parmigiano-Reggiano cheese, for serving

½ cup croutons, for serving

F·A·L·L *(aka Football)*

Sometimes I feel like a foreign exchange student in Water Valley, especially when folks are talking football. You may care passionately about the game, like Dixie and just about everybody I know, or it may barely be on your radar, as it is for Kagan and me. But regardless, if you live in a small town in the Deep South, football will shape your life during the fall.

Friday nights during the fall are about high school football. An air of excitement fills the town all day long, and then in the evening, as folks get off work, the volume of traffic on Main Street picks up rather than tapering off as it usually does. People speed to the football field, where they fill the bleachers, buy nachos from the Booster Club, let their kids run wild, and gossip in the stands as boys in blue and white run up and down.

Saturdays are about college ball. In these parts, that means Ole Miss, specifically. There are many, many thousands of ardent fans of this team, and Dixie sure is one of them. She watches every game in her living room and manages to attend a few in person every season. If the Rebels win, she's lit up for days, like everybody else in this obsessed town.

I don't care if the Rebels win or lose, but I do know their schedule. Home games mean that everyone in town is buying food for parties at home or to take up to the Grove—a vast expanse of lawn dotted with immense trees that's situated in the middle of the campus, which on game weekends is the site of a massive tailgate. Once the game starts, anybody left in Water Valley is inside, glued to their television sets. The town will go from bustling in the morning to strangely, eerily silent in the afternoon until the game finishes a few hours later.

All this reverence for America's most iconic game means that—locally, at least—football players are major celebrities. Even the high school stars, like Cora's nephews Hunter and Taylor, and our afternoon cashier, D. J. Jones, get a lot of back patting and special treatment. For one, Dixie makes all those boys huge club sandwiches whenever they come in for lunch. Are club sandwiches on the menu? Nope. I haven't ever asked Dixie for a club sandwich, but I'm pretty sure if I do, she'll ask me if I'm a football player.

Mr. Wayne, husband to one of my favorite customers, has yet to confess to me his football past, but this being a small town, I've found out about it anyway. He is married to Cheryl, who has shopped with us since we opened our doors and is absolutely one of my top five favorites. She is a pretty, petite lady with short blonde hair who is way cooler than you'd think a middle-aged special ed teacher would be.

One day, Cheryl got to telling me about how her husband had lost a whole bunch of weight—as in fifty pounds. And then somebody else said something about how Mr. Wayne used to be a big-time football star. So when he came stomping into the store at some point in his huge work boots, in a hurry for a bologna sandwich and some hot coffee, I asked him about it. He smiled at me and said, "Not really." And then Dixie handed him his bologna sandwich, and I asked him for $3.75. (He got coffee, remember.)

Later on, Danny Edwards, a story in his own right, told me Mr. Wayne was a three-year all-SEC pick in college who went on to start for the New Jersey Generals. So yeah, he was a big-time football player. Don't ask him, though.

WILD MUSHROOM SOUP *with Sherry*

SERVES 6 TO 8

I met Kagan when I was eighteen. He was nineteen. We are kind of cousins. (His aunt and my uncle met in college, cohabited for decades, married briefly, divorced. When we were engaged, Kagan would refer to my uncle Mike as his once and future uncle.)

We didn't date for a couple of years, but when we finally got together and were discovering all the reasons we were well suited for each other, we found, to our completely mutual delight, that we both really like mushrooms.

My mother says Kagan and I are dangerous together. I can see her point: Before we became a couple, the craziest thing I ever did was dye streaks of my hair green at poetry camp, making sure that it would wash out by the time school started. Then I met Kagan, and with him, everything in the world seems possible. Sure, we can build a cabin in the woods! Have children! Open a store! One night, with a bottle of wine and a corporate performance bonus, we were an inch away from buying a decrepit wreck of a house in southern France over the Internet. We've never actually been to southern France, but hey! What could go wrong, right?

Seven years, several buildings, two children, and multiple acts of lunacy later, we both still like mushrooms. If you like mushrooms, you will love this soup. If you do not like mushrooms, you will not.

½ cup (1 stick) unsalted butter

½ cup extra-virgin olive oil

1 medium yellow onion, chopped (1½ cups)

1 large leek (white part only), well rinsed and chopped (1 cup)

1 bay leaf

½ pound cremini mushrooms, sliced

½ pound button mushrooms, sliced

½ pound chanterelle mushrooms sliced

½ pound shiitake mushrooms, sliced

1 garlic clove, chopped

½ cup cognac or brandy

8 cups Chicken Stock, homemade (page 45) or store-bought, or vegetable stock

1 tablespoon chopped fresh rosemary

1 tablespoon chopped fresh thyme

1 teaspoon freshly ground black pepper

4 cups heavy cream

1 cup good sherry (Dixie likes Harveys Bristol Cream), plus more for serving

Salt

In an 8-quart stockpot set over medium heat, heat the butter and oil. Add the onion, leek, and bay leaf and cook, stirring, until the onion and leeks are soft and translucent, 10 minutes. Add the mushrooms and garlic, reduce the heat to medium-low, and cook until soft, 10 minutes. Add the cognac and cook until it has evaporated, 5 minutes. Add the stock, rosemary, thyme, and pepper. Bring to a simmer and cook until thick and creamy, 1 hour.

Stir in the cream and sherry, season with salt to taste, bring the soup back to a simmer, and cook for 15 to 20 more minutes. Remove the bay leaf.

Serve in bowls, drizzled with a little more sherry.

ROASTED PUMPKIN SOUP

1 (15-ounce) can pumpkin puree

¼ cup extra-virgin olive oil

2 tablespoons unsalted butter

1 small yellow onion, finely
chopped (½ cup)

1 shallot, finely chopped

2 tablespoons minced peeled fresh
ginger

2 garlic cloves, chopped

¼ cup Myers's dark rum

1 cup Chicken Stock, homemade
(page 45) or store-bought

1 cup apple juice

2 tablespoons honey

1 tablespoon fresh lime juice

1 teaspoon ground cinnamon

½ teaspoon ground allspice

SERVES 4

One autumn day, I walked into the kitchen and asked Dixie what soup she was making. "Pumpkin," she said.

And I thought to myself, Pumpkin? That sounds gross. I don't really want to eat that. I did not say this, however, because Dixie is fierce when provoked. Instead, I helped myself to a small cup when the lunch rush had died down.

"This is really good," I said.

"Mm-hmm," Dixie said, and continued doing whatever she does behind her sandwich table.

I am not the only skeptic eating my words.

Danny Edwards is a grizzled blue-eyed man generally wearing camouflage and a hat. He drinks beer and whiskey (so I hear), drives an odd little truck, has a round tin of tobacco in his pocket, knows everyone in town. He's been coming to the B.T.C. since the day we opened. Why, I don't know. He didn't used to buy anything except black coffee. When we first opened, we had a seventy-five-cents-a-cup policy if you brought your own mug. But Danny's mug was so small, and he doesn't even use cream or sugar, so we let him buy it at fifty cents a cup. Those prices are long gone (now it's a dollar with your cup!), but he's grandfathered into fifty cents.

Day in and day out, it's a good bet Danny will swing through the back door and say, "How ya doing, girls?" But since Dixie came, something else happened: Danny occasionally buys himself breakfast or lunch.

Tell the truth, I wasn't sure Dixie and Danny would get along. Sure, they're both old-school Mississippi, but Dixie's a raving liberal who eats octopus and Danny's a die-hard Republican who eats squirrel.

Boy, was I wrong. They are the best of friends. Dixie doesn't even yell at the man when he calls his breakfast order in at 10:32, two minutes past her cut-off time. (I will say they sure do fight hard about politics, though.)

Anyhow, the other day, I saw Danny Edwards sitting at his customary spot, shoulders hunched over a bowl. He was eating pumpkin soup.

The world shook beneath my feet. Then he finished up, tucked a fresh pinch of chaw in his cheek, and things got back to normal.

This soup is shockingly good. Dixie dollops a little Spiced Honey Cream Cheese on the top as garnish, but it's just fine without.

Preheat the oven to 450°F.

Spread the pumpkin puree on a baking sheet. Roast for 15 minutes, until the puree starts to brown. Remove the pan from the oven and set aside.

In an 8-quart stockpot set over medium heat, heat the oil and butter. Add the onion, shallot, and ginger and cook, stirring, until soft, 10 minutes. Add the garlic and cook for 1 more minute. Add the rum and cook, stirring, until it has evaporated, 5 to 7 minutes. Add the stock, apple juice, and roasted pumpkin. Whisk until smooth, bring to a simmer, reduce the heat to low, and cook until it starts to thicken, 30 minutes. Add the honey, lime juice, cinnamon, allspice, nutmeg, anise, and turmeric. Cook for 30 more minutes. Whisk in the cream and cook for 15 more minutes.

Serve in bowls, topped with the pumpkin seeds and cream cheese, if desired.

⅛ teaspoon ground nutmeg

⅛ teaspoon ground anise

⅛ teaspoon ground turmeric

4 cups heavy cream

½ cup toasted or dry-roasted pumpkin seeds, for serving (optional)

Spiced Honey Cream Cheese (page 41), for serving (optional)

BUTTERNUT SQUASH SOUP
with Roasted Apple

SERVES 6 TO 8

If you have a butternut squash in your life, this is a perfect soup for it. Butternut squash soup is smooth and slightly sweet and slightly spicy; it's one of my favorite soups. Versatile enough to feed a baby or a sit-down dinner party. Perfect for those crisp days that smell of leaves.

Preheat the oven to 425°F.

Toss the apples in just enough oil to coat, and season with salt and pepper. Put them out on a baking sheet, cored side down, and roast for 30 to 45 minutes, until caramelized. Set aside to let cool.

In an 8-quart stockpot set over medium heat, heat the butter and oil. Add the squash and onion and cook, stirring, until the squash is soft, about 15 minutes. Add the garlic and cook for another 5 minutes. Add the roasted apples, stock, cider, vinegar, apple butter, cinnamon stick, allspice, fennel, nutmeg, and cloves. Bring the mixture up to a simmer, reduce the heat to low, and cook for about 1 hour.

Remove the pot from the heat, take out the cinnamon stick, and using an immersion blender or working in batches with a regular blender, puree until smooth.

Ladle into bowls and sprinkle with the thyme.

2 pounds Granny Smith apples, peeled, halved, and cored

2 tablespoons extra-virgin olive oil, plus more for apples

Salt

¼ teaspoon freshly ground black pepper, plus more for apples

½ cup (1 stick) unsalted butter

6 pounds butternut squash, peeled, seeded, and chopped

1 large yellow onion, chopped (2 cups)

1 garlic clove, chopped

8 cups Chicken Stock, homemade (page 45) or store-bought, or vegetable stock

2 cups fresh apple cider

2 tablespoons apple cider vinegar (Dixie prefers the Bragg brand)

2 tablespoons apple butter

1 small cinnamon stick

⅛ teaspoon ground allspice

⅛ teaspoon ground fennel

⅛ teaspoon ground nutmeg

Dash of ground cloves

A few sprigs fresh thyme

HOTTY TODDY BEER CHILI

SERVES 8

2 tablespoons extra-virgin olive oil

1 medium Vidalia onion, finely chopped

1 medium red bell pepper, cored, seeded, and finely chopped

2 pounds ground chuck

1 garlic clove, minced

¼ cup dry red wine

8 cups beef stock

1 bottle Negra Modelo beer

1 (14.5-ounce) can hot chili beans in sauce

1 (14.5-ounce) can pinto beans, rinsed and drained

1 (10-ounce) can Ro-Tel tomatoes

1 (14.5-ounce) can diced fire-roasted tomatoes, drained

Juice of 1 lime

1 (8-ounce) can tomato sauce

1 (6-ounce) can tomato paste

1 teaspoon Worcestershire sauce

1 teaspoon ketchup

6 to 8 dashes Tabasco sauce

6 to 8 dashes Texas Pete hot sauce

2 tablespoons ground cumin

1 tablespoon chili powder

1 tablespoon granulated garlic

1 tablespoon granulated onion

1 tablespoon onion powder

SERVES 8

As a grocer, I'm constantly looking for patterns in food buying. There are more than you might think: On rainy days, everyone wants to eat breakfast, for some reason. If it's a beautiful Saturday, odds are good we'll have a slow lunch.

But beyond the tribal patterns, I like to keep track of individuals, too. We have no store cards keeping track of your buying history at the B.T.C. There's just me and my brain to remember to point out kale to Megan and Matt, or blue cheese to Melissa, or chocolate pies to Miss Virginia.

Miss Marilyn calls in take-out orders for pimento cheese sandwiches quite a bit, to the point where we just write "4 Marilyns to go" on a ticket (classic pimento cheese, extra mayo, lettuce, white bread). If she calls on a day we are serving Hotty Toddy chili, I make sure to let her know. Topped with shredded cheese and sour cream, this chili is one of our best-selling soups, and it's perfect for football season.

In an 8-quart stockpot set over medium heat, heat the oil. Add the onion and bell pepper and cook, stirring, until soft, 10 minutes. Add the chuck, garlic, and red wine and cook until the meat is brown throughout, 15 to 20 minutes. Add the stock, beer, chili beans, pinto beans, Ro-Tel tomatoes, fire-roasted tomatoes, and lime juice. Bring to a simmer and add the tomato sauce, tomato paste, Worcestershire sauce, ketchup, Tabasco, Texas Pete, cumin, chili powder, granulated garlic, granulated onion, onion powder, paprika, cornmeal, sugar, pepper, and cinnamon. Reduce the heat to low and cook until thickened, 2½ to 3 hours. Season with salt to taste.

To serve, ladle the soup into bowls and serve with the crushed tortilla chips, cheese, sour cream, olives, avocado, lime wedges, and cilantro on the side for folks to put on top as they please.

1 tablespoon sweet paprika

1 tablespoon cornmeal

⅛ teaspoon sugar

⅛ teaspoon freshly ground black pepper

Dash of ground cinnamon

Salt

Optional toppings

4 cups crushed tortilla chips

½ pound pepper jack or Cheddar cheese, shredded (2 cups)

½ cup sour cream

½ cup chopped black olives

4 avocados, pitted and sliced (½ avocado per bowl)

8 lime wedges

Leaves from 1 bunch cilantro

Salads

VETRA'S THREE-BEAN SALAD

BROCCOLI SALAD

APPLE SALAD

ENGLISH PEA SALAD

CUCUMBER TOMATO SALAD

WARM BRUSSELS SPROUTS SALAD

WATERMELON SALAD *with* FETA

MUSTARD DILL POTATO SALAD

MACARONI SALAD

EGG *and* OLIVE SALAD

DIXIE DALE'S SHRIMP SALAD

B.T.C. TUNA SALAD

DIXIE'S FAMOUS CHICKEN SALAD

B.T.C. CAESAR SALAD

ASPARAGUS *and* STRAWBERRY SALAD

ITALIAN CHEF SALAD

VIETNAMESE SALAD *with* CARROT-GINGER-LIME
VINAIGRETTE

SPINACH SALAD

VETRA'S THREE-BEAN SALAD

SERVES 6

Three-bean salad is pure comfort food. It may not be the most surprising dish at a potluck, but we all know it, and sometimes, in these days of arugula and radicchio, that's a good and worthwhile thing. Dixie actually abhors three-bean salad but makes it for others with the understanding that no church function, potluck, or funeral would be complete without it. I love and adore three-bean salad and recommend making a big batch during summertime for lunches, dinners, and impromptu picnics. Tastes better the longer it sits in the refrigerator.

In a large bowl, combine all of the beans, the onion, bell pepper, vinegar, sugar, oil, and cloves. Stir well and refrigerate for 24 hours to allow the flavors to develop.

Serve at room temperature. The salad will keep in an airtight container in the refrigerator for 4 days.

2 (14.5-ounce) cans green beans, rinsed and drained

1 (14.5-ounce) can wax beans, rinsed and drained

1 (12-ounce) can red kidney beans, rinsed and drained

1 small yellow onion, thinly sliced (½ cup)

1 small red bell pepper, cored, seeded, and thinly sliced (½ cup)

1 cup white vinegar

1 cup sugar

½ cup vegetable oil

½ teaspoon ground cloves

BROCCOLI SALAD

SERVES 8

8 cups fresh broccoli florets

1 cup mayonnaise

2 teaspoons sugar

½ teaspoon kosher salt

1 teaspoon freshly ground black pepper

¼ pound Cheddar cheese, shredded (1 cup)

½ small purple onion, finely chopped (¼ cup)

4 strips cooked bacon, chopped (about ¼ cup)

¼ cup dried cranberries

¼ cup golden raisins

I wish my children were the types to eat tofu, crawfish, and kale, but they're not. They are mired in the picky years between three and six, and though they happily eat their weight in fresh fruit, green vegetables are a dubious proposition. Broccoli is the exception. They prefer it raw. I should encourage the habit, I know, but raw broccoli smacks of those bland supermarket vegetable trays that you eat from at parties when you're trying to be virtuous.

This salad turns broccoli into something entirely unvirtuous. It is the lush-hipped Sophia Loren of the vegetable salad world and absolutely irresistible.

Fill a medium pot with water, set it over high heat, and bring it to a rolling boil. Add the broccoli and cook until it is bright green but still crisp, 3 minutes. Drain well.

In a small bowl, combine the mayonnaise, sugar, salt, and pepper.

In a separate bowl, combine the cheese, onion, bacon, cranberries, and raisins. Add the broccoli. Gently fold in the mayonnaise mixture until evenly mixed. Cover and refrigerate for 4 hours before serving.

The salad will keep in an airtight container in the refrigerator for 3 days.

APPLE SALAD

1 cup Hellmann's mayonnaise

¼ cup fresh lemon juice

2 tablespoons honey

⅛ teaspoon white pepper

5 pounds Granny Smith apples, cored and sliced

1 cup halved seedless red grapes

3 celery hearts (including leaves), finely chopped (½ cup)

⅛ teaspoon celery seeds

Salt

Oh, apples. Dixie and the other B.T.C. girls make fun of me for my love for apples. When you enter the B.T.C., one of the first things you see is the apple cart, an old sweet potato crate divided into four sections, each heaped with a different variety of apples.

Once upon a time, Virginia was known for its apples, and the tradition lingers in the neck of the woods I'm from. Fall meant trips to the orchard down the road and gallons of fresh cider from the mill—the unpasteurized kind that fermented after a few days, so you had to drink it quick. Man, that stuff is good.

This salad tastes fresh and light and has great crunch. We sell it as a side dish during holidays, and it's worth noting that the apples, thanks to the lemon juice, hold up well, ensuring that you can make this ahead of time and not have to worry about poor presentation.

In a large glass bowl, combine the mayonnaise, lemon juice, honey, and white pepper. Add the apples, grapes, celery, and celery seeds, and season with salt to taste. Toss well. Refrigerate overnight.

Serve cold. The salad will keep in an airtight container in the refrigerator for 3 days.

Where Food Comes From

EVERY WEEK, sometimes twice, I drive fifty miles one way to an unassuming metal warehouse set behind a rickety wooden shack festooned with bags of peanuts and turnip greens on ice. This is my produce wholesaler: a place where the three fellows who run it buy directly from farmers all across the USA. Because of this establishment, the B.T.C. can lay its hands on imported bananas, Arizona cantaloupes, Florida tomatoes, and in the fall, Alabama and even Virginia apples. I buy produce from many other places and local farmers, but my business could not dependably exist without this warehouse. When I first opened the B.T.C., I did not know of their existence.

If you're like me—a person to whom the word *wholesale* barely meant anything—opening a business has some challenges. There is no handy-dandy Yellow Pages of wholesalers, and most of them do not have a web presence. Instead, you just have to know, or know someone who knows, and back in 2010, I didn't.

I found my produce wholesaler because my old buddy Wilbur Herring, a man with a nose for a deal, told me about the crazy-low produce prices that exist in a produce shack over in the town of Pontotoc. One day, shortly after the store opened, I was driving around in that neck of the woods picking up tomatoes from the Amish farmers, and I took a quick detour to check the place out.

The prices are crazy low. About half of what a supermarket charges. I asked the lady behind the counter if they wholesaled, a term I had recently learned, which basically means sell more for less without sales tax, and she said, "Yeah, hon. Go to the warehouse out back."

Ever since that day, I back my van up to the concrete pad next to the warehouse a couple times a week, and Brandon or Billy Wayne runs around with a pallet jack, checking my items off a clipboard and loading them into my van while I wheedle 'em to go faster, because I'm always late.

I like three things about my produce wholesaler. One, their prices. I can compete with the big guys because these folks are so reasonable. Two, their business philosophy: They buy imported Chilean fruit, like all wholesalers, but they also buy from the Amish farmers who live nine miles south. It's not unusual to see a horse and buggy tethered to the magnolia tree out front. They buy apricots from California and Japanese persimmons from somewhere and apples from all over the country. Georgia peaches and Louisiana strawberries and Texas grapefruit. And the third thing I like?

Produce. Something about rows of gleaming fruits and vegetables gets my heart pumping. In terms of sales, produce isn't always really worth the time or energy for the B.T.C., not unless it's April through August. But no matter what my store evolves into, we will always, always sell fruits and vegetables, and I will always, always cluck over the new apples. Arkansas Black. Winesap. Black Twig. Mutsu. Oh, apple season.

ENGLISH PEA SALAD

SERVES 8

I'd never heard of English peas before I moved to Mississippi and began hanging out with farmers. Turns out they mean what my mama just called peas: the sweet green peas commonly found canned or frozen.

This salad reminds me of one that my Pennsylvanian nana used to make. She was a wonderful cook and a complete eccentric who was as well known for her skinny-dipping and airplane flying as her dinner parties. I liked her salad so much during my childhood that I asked her for the recipe when I was in college. Sadly, I lost it and she passed on, so I've never had the chance to compare the two. But Dixie's tastes like my nana's with one exception: bacon. When I make it, I add bacon, like my nana did. Hard to go wrong with bacon.

Soul food seasoning is a spice mix that you'll find in most grocery store spice aisles. Dixie's recipe calls for canned peas for year-round convenience, but if you happen to find fresh peas at your farmers' market in early spring, use those instead!

In a large bowl, combine the cheese, eggs, bell pepper, onion, pimiento, mayonnaise, sour cream, vinegar, basil, sugar, soul food seasoning, granulated garlic, parsley, pepper, and Tabasco. Stir in the peas and refrigerate overnight.

Serve at room temperature. The salad will keep in an airtight container in the refrigerator for 5 days.

2 ounces Cheddar cheese, shredded (½ cup)

2 hard-boiled eggs, grated

1 small yellow bell pepper, cored, seeded, and finely chopped (½ cup)

2 tablespoons finely chopped red onion

2 teaspoons chopped pimiento

½ cup Hellmann's mayonnaise

½ cup sour cream

1 teaspoon apple cider vinegar (Dixie prefers the Bragg brand)

3 tablespoons dried basil

1 teaspoon sugar

1 teaspoon soul food seasoning

1 teaspoon granulated garlic

1 teaspoon chopped fresh parsley

½ teaspoon freshly ground black pepper

2 dashes Tabasco sauce

4 (14.5-ounce) cans baby peas, drained (Dixie prefers Le Sueur brand)

CUCUMBER TOMATO SALAD

SERVES 4

1 large burpless cucumber, peeled, halved lengthwise, and thinly sliced

2 large homegrown tomatoes, cored and cut into small wedges

½ Vidalia onion, thinly sliced

¼ cup extra-virgin olive oil

¼ cup apple cider vinegar (Dixie prefers the Bragg brand)

¼ cup sugar

½ teaspoon chopped fresh dill

½ teaspoon freshly ground black pepper

1 teaspoon salt

I have a complicated relationship with tomatoes, maybe more complicated than most.

To begin with, I abhorred them as a child. Couldn't stand the taste; none of us could. So my poor mother would grow them every summer, slice them up, put them on the table, and watch every member of her family turn their nose up at her hard work. How this did not break her heart, I will never know.

For another, my father's clan in Pennsylvania is part of a long and strange saga where every Labor Day, we and about three hundred other weirdos get together and throw tomatoes at each other. The Tomato War is a decades-long and very serious tradition. There are two armies, two generals, declarations of war, and so forth, and on Labor Day morning, hordes of screaming WASPs are running through the woods, throwing tomatoes at each other. If you get hit, you're dead, and you tie a white strip of fabric around your arm and trudge off to the graveyard, a designated area in a field somewhere where you drink beer or sip from a flask or, if underage, help yourself to birch beer from a metal keg. Then you jump in a lake.

Anyhow.

A classic and very uncomplicated thing to do in summertime is to make cucumber-tomato salad. It is easy, crisp, refreshing, perfect with some good bread to mop up the juices with.

In a large bowl, combine the cucumber, tomatoes, onion, oil, vinegar, sugar, dill, pepper, and salt. Toss well, cover the bowl, and chill in the refrigerator overnight.

Serve at room temperature. The salad will keep in an airtight container in the refrigerator for 3 days.

WARM BRUSSELS SPROUTS SALAD

SERVES 4

Before Kagan and I moved to Mississippi, we knew nothing about it. I had so little idea of what life in Mississippi was like that I wasn't quite sure if the state had winter.

It turns out that it does.

It's shorter, for one thing; December through February, though daffodils often begin blooming in February. And though we've had snow, it's always gone by midday. But it is heat-on, jacket-wearing, leaves-off-the-trees winter nonetheless, and so we get our chance to roast chestnuts and put the kids in adorable hats with pompoms as is our God-given Yankee right.

Which brings me to Brussels sprouts, one of winter's produce highlights (along with satsumas and Meyer lemons and yes, kale). I actually adore Brussels sprouts. So does Dixie. But at some point in her culinary career, she was so tired of boiling and sautéing and roasting the little cabbages that she created this dish: a warm salad that includes bacon, and is a wondrous thing to eat on a chilly day in any part of the country.

2 tablespoons extra-virgin olive oil

1 shallot, chopped

¼ pound prosciutto, chopped

1 pound Brussels sprouts, sliced

⅛ teaspoon freshly ground black pepper

½ cup walnuts

¼ cup dried cranberries

¼ cup golden raisins

1 tablespoon malt vinegar

2 tablespoons Madeira

Salt

In a large skillet or sauté pan set over medium heat, heat the oil. Add the shallot and prosciutto and cook, stirring, until the shallot is soft, 3 minutes. Add the Brussels sprouts and pepper and cook, stirring, until the spouts become bright green, 5 minutes. Add the walnuts, dried cranberries, raisins, and vinegar and cook until the sprouts are tender, 5 minutes. Add the Madeira and cook, stirring, for 2 more minutes. Season with salt to taste.

Serve warm.

WATERMELON SALAD *with* FETA

SERVES 6

6 cups cubed watermelon, seeds removed

1 cup crumbled feta cheese

½ medium purple onion, thinly sliced (½ cup)

¼ cup thinly sliced fresh mint

¼ cup extra-virgin olive oil

¼ cup honey

1 teaspoon kosher salt

1 teaspoon freshly ground black pepper

½ cup balsamic vinegar

It's impossible to overstate how wondrous this salad is. Savory, sweet, with a plethora of textures, it is the absolute perfect summer supper all by itself or a great side dish. I have been known to eat it standing up in the middle of a hot, steamy night straight from the container, and how many salads can you say that about?

In a large bowl, gently toss together the watermelon, feta, onion, mint, oil, honey, salt, and pepper.

Put the balsamic vinegar in a saucepan set over medium-high heat. Cook until the liquid has reduced by half and is thick like syrup, about 15 minutes. Let cool slightly.

Drizzle the balsamic reduction over the salad and serve immediately. This salad does not hold well, so serve within the hour of making it.

MUSTARD DILL POTATO SALAD

In this day and age of wondrous food from exotic locales, it can be easy to forget that American staples like potato or macaroni salad exist for a reason: They're good. This particular potato salad is heavy on flavor, classic enough for the potato salad purists in your life, and good to eat as a side with everything from grilled sausages to BBQ to fried chicken. Or you could keep it simple and pair it with a watermelon and a warm summer day somewhere breezy.

Boil the potatoes in salted water for 20 minutes, or until fork-tender. Drain well and transfer to a large bowl. Let cool for 20 minutes.

While the potatoes are still warm, add the celery, onion, mayonnaise, mustard, egg, dill and sweet relishes, pimientos, vinegar, dill, sugar, paprika, pepper, and salt. Toss with your hands, breaking up some of the potatoes as you go, until mixed well. Cover and chill in the refrigerator overnight.

Serve cold. The salad will keep in an airtight container in the refrigerator for 5 days.

3 pounds red potatoes, quartered

3 celery hearts, finely chopped (½ cup)

1 teaspoon grated yellow onion

1½ cups Hellmann's mayonnaise

¼ cup yellow mustard

6 hard-boiled eggs, grated

4 teaspoons dill pickle relish

4 teaspoons sweet pickle relish

1 (4-ounce jar) chopped pimientos, drained

¼ cup apple cider vinegar (Dixie prefers the Bragg brand)

2 tablespoons chopped fresh dill

2 tablespoons sugar

½ teaspoon sweet paprika

½ teaspoon freshly ground black pepper

1 teaspoon salt

MACARONI SALAD

1 pound elbow macaroni

4 celery hearts, finely chopped

2 medium carrots, grated (1 cup)

1 cup chopped sweet pickles

½ small onion, grated

1 (4-ounce) jar chopped pimientos, drained

6 hard-boiled eggs, grated

2 cups Hellmann's mayonnaise

½ cup Dijon mustard (Dixie prefers Grey Poupon)

1 tablespoon apple cider vinegar (Dixie prefers the Bragg brand)

4 dashes Tabasco sauce

2 tablespoons chopped fresh parsley

2 tablespoons granulated garlic

4 teaspoons sugar

2 teaspoons freshly ground black pepper

1 teaspoon dry mustard

Salt

As with all pasta salads, the most important thing is to remember to add the cooked macaroni to the mayo mixture while still warm, so the noodles absorb all the ingredients and flavors.

This particular macaroni salad is as classic Americana as they come. Make as a trio: the Cucumber Tomato Salad (page 88), this, and perhaps Vetra's Three-Bean Salad (page 81), and have a light dinner, preferably outside.

Cook the macaroni according to the package instructions. Drain well and set aside.

In a large bowl, combine the celery, carrots, pickles, onion, pimientos, eggs, mayonnaise, Dijon mustard, vinegar, Tabasco, parsley, granulated garlic, sugar, pepper, and dry mustard. Season with salt to taste. Add the cooked macaroni and toss until well coated. Refrigerate overnight.

Serve cold. The salad will keep in an airtight container in the refrigerator for 5 days.

EGG *and* OLIVE SALAD

SERVES 4

Another Southern staple that, according to my customers, folks elsewhere don't eat. That's quite a shame, because it's high in protein and in satisfaction. Perfect served simply with crackers, it's also divine made into a sandwich on toasted white bread with bacon and tomato.

In a large bowl, combine the eggs, olives, mayonnaise, mustard, granulated onion, granulated garlic, white pepper, sugar, and Tabasco. Mix well, cover the bowl with plastic wrap, and chill in the refrigerator overnight.

Serve cold. The salad will keep in an airtight container in the refrigerator for 4 days.

13 hard-boiled eggs, grated

1 cup chopped green olives

1 cup Hellmann's mayonnaise

1 tablespoon yellow mustard

1 teaspoon granulated onion

1 teaspoon granulated garlic

½ teaspoon white pepper

½ teaspoon sugar

Dash of Tabasco sauce

DIXIE DALE'S SHRIMP SALAD

SERVES 4 TO 6

Three Mississippi state governors and one Morgan Freeman have enjoyed this shrimp salad. (One of the aforementioned told Dixie it was the best thing he'd ever put in his mouth.)

Whenever make-ahead elegance is called for—think baby showers, christenings, informal afternoon weddings—make this recipe. It keeps well for several days in the refrigerator, looks beautiful, and wows its audience. Dixie serves it on a bed of lettuce with sliced avocado, tomato, and lemon wedges.

If you happened to be a young lady getting married in Water Valley, Mississippi, your church would throw you a tea, and some variation on this would be served on a crystal platter that had likely been purchased at Turnage Drug Store.

1 cup Old Bay seasoning

1 pound shrimp

4 cups Hellmann's mayonnaise

Juice of 2 lemons

2 tablespoons dry white wine or dry vermouth

2 tablespoons Dijon mustard

2 teaspoons Worcestershire sauce

3 dashes Tabasco sauce

½ cup finely chopped green onions

3 celery hearts, finely chopped (½ cup)

2 tablespoons chopped fresh parsley

4 teaspoons garlic salt

¼ teaspoon cayenne pepper

½ teaspoon sweet paprika

½ teaspoon white pepper

Bring 6 cups of water and the Old Bay to a boil in a 4-quart stockpot set over high heat. Add the shrimp and cook until they start to curl and turn pink, 3 minutes. Using a mesh strainer, transfer the shrimp to a bowl of ice water. Let sit for 2 minutes, drain the shrimp, and then put them on paper towels to dry. Peel, devein, and chop the shrimp.

In a large bowl, combine the mayonnaise, lemon juice, wine, mustard, Worcestershire sauce, Tabasco, onions, celery, parsley, garlic salt, cayenne, paprika, and white pepper.

About 30 minutes before you're ready to serve the salad, add the shrimp and return the bowl to the refrigerator.

Serve when chilled. The salad will keep in an airtight container in the refrigerator for 3 days.

Turnage Drug Store and Water Valley Weddings

TURNER DRUG STORE is a fourth-generation pharmacy that still has a soda fountain and booths and serves up a wicked Purple Cow. In addition to dispensing medications and milkshakes, the drugstore serves as Water Valley's unofficial department store. Couples register for a selection of the stemware, crystal, and silver that the drugstore carries. We at the B.T.C. have a special fondness for Turnage because Cora, our baker, is a Turnage herself. Plus, whenever we run out of quarters during non-bank hours, they help us out. Since Cora works with us and all.

But beyond being business kin, Turnage is an amazing place to shop. When Eddie and Pat Ray's daughter Nancy Margaret became engaged, I went down and picked out a crystal bowl for her wedding shower the Methodist church was hosting. Much to my delight, Mrs. Jo, the pharmacist's wife, said the drugstore would take care of wrapping and delivering the item to the church tea, along with a note saying it was from me. All I had to do was point at the bowl and write a check.

Two months later, I got a very polite thank-you note from Nancy Margaret, whose gorgeous fairy-tale wedding included gospel singers on a balcony who repeatedly sang "What a Friend We Have" over and over again, omitting "Jesus," because Nancy Margaret's groom is of Jewish heritage. True story.

B.T.C. TUNA SALAD

1½ cups Hellmann's mayonnaise

4 (7-ounce) cans albacore tuna in water, well drained

3 celery hearts, finely chopped (½ cup)

2 tablespoons golden raisins

2 tablespoons brown raisins

4 hard-boiled eggs, grated

¼ cup sweet pickle relish

2 tablespoons dill pickle relish

½ teaspoon granulated onion

½ teaspoon granulated garlic

½ teaspoon freshly ground black pepper

Dash of Tabasco sauce

Salt

MAKES 4 TO 6 CUPS

Tuna salad is something that many rich people don't eat (they eat chicken salad, three dollars per pound more). But working within the medium of the economical tuna, something beautiful has emerged. It's still tuna salad, mind you. But it is savory and a delicious thing when served on a bed of greens with crackers on the side, or—my go-to on busy days when I need something to get me through—toasted bread with spinach as a sandwich. Also, in the post-Thanksgiving season, tuna salad is shockingly good with B.T.C. Cranberry Sauce (page 121) in a wrap.

In a large bowl, combine the mayonnaise, tuna, celery, golden and brown raisins, eggs, sweet and dill relishes, granulated onion, granulated garlic, pepper, and Tabasco. Season with salt to taste.

This salad is best if chilled overnight, but you can also serve it immediately. It will keep in an airtight container in the refrigerator for 4 days.

DIXIE'S FAMOUS CHICKEN SALAD

SERVES 6

The thing that takes a while to get used to in Mississippi is there is no "six degrees of separation." Instead, it's more like six hundred half degrees of absolutely no separation whatsoever. This means that you can never flip somebody the bird when they cut you off in traffic (not that that happens anyway, but there are numerous elderly in large metallic sedans who cannot see you or, indeed, the road). You cannot criticize anybody to anyone else, because whoever you critique will invariably be your audience's cousin or best friend or something. I promise.

And it means that stories can take a while to tell.

So, in a cute yellow house on a shady street in town live Jaime and Alida. Both English professors at Ole Miss, they work in Oxford but live in Water Valley. We've run into each other at the farmers' market, while dog walking, and at gallery receptions. (Incidentally, they bought their house from Eddie, the handsome farmer who gives me free okra.) It turns out that Alida is also one of Dixie's oldest friends. When Dixie was exiting Texas and a difficult period of her life, Alida and Jaime are the ones who swooped in like the Nascar-loving angels they are and carried her back to Mississippi.

And so it was Alida to whom Dixie said, "You know, I think I'll make chicken salad at the store this week." And it is Alida, who understands Mississippians' obsession with the substance, who said, "You're going to regret it if you do."

Dixie ignored Alida's advice. She made her chicken salad. And now she regrets it, because every day of every week, somebody wants to know when Dixie is going to make it again.

Meat from 1 Boiled Chicken (page 45)

8 hard-boiled eggs, grated

6 celery hearts, finely chopped (1 cup)

1 (8-ounce) jar Mt. Olive sweet pickle relish

2 tablespoons dill pickle relish

4 cups Hellmann's mayonnaise

1 tablespoon balsamic vinegar

Juice of 1 lemon

1 tablespoon granulated garlic

1 tablespoon granulated onion

1 teaspoon freshly ground black pepper

Salt

Note

The key to getting this right is to mix up the salad while the chicken is still warm, because it absorbs the flavors better. Work it with your hands, which helps break up the chicken properly and allows the seasonings to get into it. And, as with most salads, a stay in the refrigerator overnight helps, too.

While the chicken is still warm, put it in a large bowl and add the eggs, celery, sweet and dill relishes, mayonnaise, vinegar, lemon juice, granulated garlic, granulated onion, and pepper. Using your hands, mix thoroughly. Season with salt to taste. You can serve it immediately, but it's best if you refrigerate it overnight.

The salad will keep in an airtight container in the refrigerator for 5 days.

B.T.C. CAESAR SALAD

SERVES 4

DRESSING

3 anchovy fillets

1 shallot

1 garlic clove

2 tablespoons fresh lemon juice

1 cup Hellmann's mayonnaise

1 tablespoon Dijon mustard

1 tablespoon Worcestershire sauce

1 tablespoon white wine vinegar

1 tablespoon dry white wine

2 tablespoons grated Parmigiano-Reggiano cheese

1 teaspoon freshly ground black pepper

½ teaspoon sugar

Salt

SALAD

3 hearts of romaine, chopped

½ cup canned sliced black olives

½ cup chopped artichoke hearts, canned

¼ cup dried cranberries

½ cup grated Parmigiano-Reggiano cheese

2 hard-boiled eggs, quartered, for serving

½ cup croutons, for serving

It's easy to tell when fall rolls in around here. Up north, they'd call it summer—fifty-something-degree nights, eighty-something-degree days—but there's a sense of relief that it's possible to go outside without wishing you hadn't. The whole town is out walking, getting ice cream, doing lawn work. The dogs (there are a lot of dogs in Mississippi) have a bounce in their step and are out ransacking garbage cans. And soccer starts, so twice a week Kagan and I hustle our kids into shin guards and take them to the park so they can twirl on the field, staring at the sky and running like maniacs during the rest breaks.

Our son's soccer coach is a good-looking nurse whose name is Allison. I was glad to have learned her real name, because I previously knew her only as Caesar Salad Nurse, who called every Friday to see if we were running the Caesar as our special.

Dixie puts all kinds of stuff into this salad not traditionally associated with Caesar salads. It looks so fine plated that when we carry one out, folks' heads swivel. And while people first question the combination of cranberries and olives, they inevitably fall hard for this delicious salad.

For the dressing, in a food processor, puree the anchovies, shallot, garlic, and lemon juice; set aside.

In a medium bowl, combine the mayonnaise, mustard, Worcestershire sauce, vinegar, wine, Parmigiano-Reggiano, pepper, and sugar. Add the anchovy mixture, season with salt to taste, and mix well. Cover the bowl and chill in the refrigerator overnight. (The dressing will keep in an airtight container in the refrigerator for up to 4 days.)

For the salad, in a large chilled bowl, combine the romaine, olives, artichoke hearts, dried cranberries, and Parmigiano-Reggiano. Add the dressing and toss lightly but thoroughly.

Divide the salad among 4 plates. Put 2 egg wedges and a few croutons on top of each, and serve immediately.

ASPARAGUS *and* STRAWBERRY *Salad*

SERVES 4 TO 6

Every spring, there exists an absolutely perfect moment in time when the late asparagus and the first strawberries coexist. This salad is one of the many wondrous dishes you can make with those two prized ingredients.

Last year, I made one of my weekly forays to the Amish settlement fifty miles from the B.T.C., forgetting that it was a Tuesday. See, Ure and Mary don't pick strawberries on Tuesday. They pick tomatoes, corn, cucumbers, white and ruby-fleshed onions, five-gallon buckets of yellow squash. But strawberries are Mondays, Wednesdays, and Fridays only.

Mary told me her brother picks strawberries on Tuesdays, and so I drove another mile down through a pine forest that suddenly opened up to a small farm. The fields on either side of the dirt road were planted in neat rows of strawberries, which I could see shining in the morning sun.

Mary's brother is a fairly new farmer and his distribution system has yet to reach Mary's meticulous precision, so he didn't yet have the berries picked and packed and sitting on the back porch. But I really wanted some strawberries. And he really wanted to sell me some. So he asked if I could wait fifteen minutes, and I said yes, and I walked after his bonneted daughters and straw-hatted sons to the fields. I squatted alongside them under the blue sky and picked berries in silence, with the occasional German word thrown out to the toddler who lurched between the plants. When the gallon containers were full, I smiled at the children, and they smiled back at me like timid deer.

It was one of the more memorable of my mornings as a grocer.

2 pounds fresh asparagus, cut on the bias (4 cups)

4 cups fresh strawberries, sliced

¼ cup extra-virgin olive oil

¼ cup balsamic vinegar

¼ cup honey

1 teaspoon kosher salt

1 teaspoon freshly ground black pepper

In an 8-quart stockpot, bring 1 cup of water to boil. Set a steaming basket on top and add the asparagus. Steam the asparagus until it is bright green and al dente, 4 to 6 minutes. Immediately transfer it to a bowl of ice water and let cool. Remove the asparagus from the bowl and pat it dry with paper towels.

Put the asparagus in a bowl and add the strawberries. In separate bowl, whisk together the oil, vinegar, honey, salt, and pepper. Pour the dressing over the asparagus strawberry mixture. Transfer to the refrigerator and chill for 1 hour before serving.

ITALIAN CHEF SALAD

SERVES 2

Sometimes people stand in front of the B.T.C.'s slice-to-order deli counter and look puzzled. The deli is our newest department and Dixie's brainchild; she scorns prepackaged prosciutto and sealed cups of olives. Folks are still getting used to the process (ring a bell, step up, place an order, peruse the rest of the store), but what we have on those three shelves is pretty impressive for a little store in a small town. We carry feta, goat cheese, mozzarella, prosciutto, sopressata, Muenster, pit-smoked ham, red-waxed wheels of hoop cheese, bologna, dill Havarti, souse (aka headcheese), liver cheese, pesto, rare roast beef, stuffed peppers, sun-cured olives, and much, much more.

This salad combines the best ingredients of a good deli and tops them with a sweet and savory dressing that makes for a hearty meal all on its own. I suggest adding to the table a deep red wine and some crusty bread, perhaps along with big-band Italian music, and maybe those candles in red jelly jars.

DRESSING

6 sweet cherry peppers, seeded and chopped

½ cup pitted Kalamata olives

½ cup pitted green Cerignola olives

½ cup chopped roasted red peppers

2 tablespoons chopped dill pickles

2 tablespoons chopped sweet pickles

2 tablespoons capers

2 tablespoons sliced jalapeños

2 garlic cloves

¼ cup extra-virgin olive oil

2 tablespoons aged balsamic vinegar

1 teaspoon freshly ground black pepper

SALAD

1 romaine heart, chopped

2 ounces prosciutto, chopped

2 ounces sopressata, chopped

2 ounces Genoa salami, chopped

2 ounces fresh mozzarella, chopped

1 ounce Parmesan cheese, shaved

1 Roma tomato, cored and chopped

1 hard-boiled egg, quartered

For the dressing, in a food processor, combine the sweet peppers, Kalamata and Cerignola olives, roasted red peppers, dill and sweet pickles, capers, jalapeños, and garlic. Pulse until finely chopped. Transfer the mixture to a medium bowl and add the oil, vinegar, and black pepper. Toss well, cover the bowl with plastic wrap, and refrigerate for 24 hours before making the salad. The dressing will keep in an airtight container in the refrigerator for 5 days.

For the salad, in a large chilled bowl, combine the romaine, prosciutto, sopressata, salami, mozzarella, Parmesan, tomato, and egg. Drizzle the dressing over the mixture and toss well.

Serve immediately. The salad will keep in an airtight container in the refrigerator for 3 days.

VIETNAMESE SALAD *with Carrot-Ginger-Lime Vinaigrette*

CARROT-GINGER-LIME VINAIGRETTE

4 carrots, chopped (2 cups)

2 garlic cloves

1 shallot, chopped

3-inch knob fresh ginger, peeled and chopped (¼ cup)

1 cup rice vinegar

¼ cup soy sauce

½ cup toasted sesame oil

¼ cup honey

2 tablespoons fresh lime juice

1 tablespoon Sriracha chili sauce

⅛ teaspoon freshly ground black pepper

Salt

SERVES 6

I have good news for you! The marinade/dressing that goes with this salad is 100 percent healthy, low-fat, and good for you! It's also shocking versatile and long-lasting: I have a bottle in my fridge that's been there for at least two months and I promise it's absolutely fine. The carrot specks don't even get funky.

The first time I tasted this vinaigrette, I wasn't even supposed to be at work. It was one of my precious days off, and Kagan had taken the opportunity to take off childless, so I had my two precious, completely obedient, and not at all ever in the slightest obnoxious children with me. Rather than staying at home and attempting to drink an uninterrupted cup of coffee while they carried the cat around, stripped all the beds to play camp, or drew on the walls, I had to take them with me to work, because the national magazine *Food & Wine* had contacted us and wanted to run a small feature on Water Valley.

Good news, yes, but despite their national presence, we didn't merit a photographer, so I had to take my own. I gave the girls a heads-up I'd be at the store on my day off, Dixie donned her chef coat and made two sexy-sounding specials, and I coerced my friends and neighbors Coulter Fussell and Megan Patton into eating said specials while I snapped their picture for a solid half hour, during which my children maniacally ate stolen Tootsie Rolls in the store's playhouse.

The upside? Dixie sent me home with one of the special Vietnamese Salads, which is so good that I literally licked the plate when I got home, as my sugar-blissed-out children shrieked in their room and jumped on their beds.

I'd also like to say *Food & Wine* did not use any of my photographs or indeed mention the fact we have a cafe at all, much to Megan and Coulter's relief and Dixie's disappointment. But the creation of this dish makes up for it. And there are lots of other things to do with this marinade, such as using it as a dipping sauce for sliced vegetables, in a stir-fry, or even as a marinade for pork or chicken before grilling. It's just that fantastic.

For the vinaigrette, in a food processor, combine the carrots, garlic, shallot, and ginger and pulse until very fine, almost like a paste. Transfer to a blender, add the vinegar, soy sauce, oil, honey, lime juice, Sriracha, and pepper, and blend for 1 minute. Season with salt to taste. You can serve it immediately, but it's best if refrigerated overnight.

For the salad, in a large bowl, combine the iceberg lettuce, spinach, carrot, bell pepper, snow peas, cucumber, mango, water chestnuts, bamboo shoots, and peanuts. Drizzle the vinaigrette over the top and toss gently by hand. Serve immediately on chilled plates.

SALAD

1 head iceberg lettuce, cored and pulled into small pieces

1 cup baby spinach, chopped

1 large carrot, julienned (¼ cup)

1 small red bell pepper, julienned (¼ cup)

¼ cup snow peas, trimmed and strings removed

1 small cucumber, peeled, seeded, and julienned (¼ cup)

1 medium ripe mango, peeled and julienned (¼ cup)

1 (8-ounce) can sliced water chestnuts, drained

1 (8-ounce) can sliced bamboo shoots, drained

½ cup Carrot-Ginger-Lime Vinaigrette

¼ cup dry-roasted salted peanuts

SPINACH SALAD

My son is smack-dab in the middle of that age where food is about power. Refusing to eat dinner is made especially challenging for him because he is a solid growing boy who can wolf down half a roast chicken and view it as a snack. Nevertheless, his obstinacy occasionally prevails: Last night he cried hysterically about the pulled pork on his plate. He loves "pig," as he calls it, but I'd made the fatal mistake of broiling some cheese on top of it . . . under which I'd hid some chopped spinach. He went to bed without dinner. (I can be pretty obstinate myself.)

Caspian tells me often about the absolutely delicious salad they serve at his nursery school. It has shredded lettuce, carrots, and purple cabbage; comes out of a bag; is drenched in nondescript ranch. He adores it.

One day, I hope he gets over his aversion to spinach, but for those of you with more aristocratic tastes than my small son, I suggest this salad. It is a crowd-pleaser, a mainstay on the B.T.C. menu, a meal in itself. Here, it is served with a balsamic dressing, but it's also great with the Buttermilk Ranch Dressing (page 128).

BALSAMIC DRESSING

6 tablespoons aged balsamic vinegar

3 tablespoons extra-virgin olive oil

Juice of 1 lemon

1 teaspoon salt

½ teaspoon freshly ground black pepper

SALAD

1 (10-ounce) bag fresh baby spinach

¼ cup walnut halves

¼ cup golden raisins

¼ cup sun-dried cranberries

¼ pound goat cheese, crumbled

4 strips crispy cooked bacon, chopped

4 hard-boiled eggs, quartered

For the dressing, put the vinegar, oil, lemon juice, salt, and pepper in a blender and blend on high for 30 seconds. The dressing will keep in an airtight container in the refrigerator for 2 weeks.

For the salad, put the spinach, walnuts, raisins, cranberries, goat cheese, and bacon in a large bowl. Using your hands, gently toss the ingredients. Divide the salad among 4 chilled serving plates.

Drizzle the balsamic dressing on top of each, add 4 egg quarters, and serve immediately.

Spreads AND *Sandwich Fixings*

RED RIND PIMENTO CHEESE

TEX-MEX PIMENTO CHEESE

HAM *and* HORSERADISH SPREAD

CLASSIC COLESLAW

SRIRACHA COLESLAW

RED CABBAGE COLESLAW *with* GOLDEN RAISINS

B.T.C. CRANBERRY SAUCE

FANCY MAYO
CHERRY MAYONNAISE
TOMATO CAPER MAYONNAISE

DIXIE *and* ANNALIESE'S ROASTED
RED PEPPER SALSA

GREEN OLIVE TAPENADE

BUTTERMILK RANCH DRESSING

THOUSAND ISLAND DRESSING

KAGAN'S DILL PICKLES

Red Rind
PIMENTO CHEESE

MAKES 4 CUPS

1 pound red rind hoop cheese, shredded (4 cups)

½ cup chopped pimientos

½ cup Hellmann's mayonnaise

1 teaspoon Worcestershire sauce

Dash of Tabasco sauce

1 teaspoon granulated onion

1 teaspoon granulated garlic

⅛ teaspoon dry mustard

⅛ teaspoon sweet paprika

⅛ teaspoon white pepper

Pinch of sugar

Salt

Pimento cheese deserves a book of its own in the South. Just about everybody down here grew up eating it. There are mass-produced tubs in the grocery stores (skip those) and every lady has her own recipe. Cora's mother puts sweet pickle and egg in hers. Coulter uses red bell peppers. As for Dixie, she actually disliked it as a child. Miss Vetra filled celery sticks and made tea sandwiches with it for church functions, and Dixie always gave it a pass.

Decades later, with mature taste buds, Dixie was making her grandmother's traditional pimento at home—and enjoying it. This recipe employs no exotic additions. Dixie recommends mixing it with your hands to get it to the perfect texture. It is wonderful on crackers and makes a fantastic sandwich, whether warm, cold, with bacon, with chicken breast and coleslaw and pickles, grilled, broiled, on toasted bread, soft bread, or croissant. There may indeed be no wrong way to eat pimento cheese.

Kagan and I were recently at one of Yalo's art openings, crammed into its former barbershop space with dozens of other people, most of whom we knew. We were in the far back, where Coulter and Megan keep their own works and works-in-progress, and Kagan was spreading pimento cheese onto crackers and eating them in the company of Coulter's circus animal series (a bear balanced on a ball gazed at us—somewhat hungrily). Kagan took a big bite and then said around a mouthful, "If anyone had told me ten years ago I'd be at an art show in Mississippi eating pimento cheese and liking it, I wouldn't have believed them."

Then he left me in the company of the bear to search for boiled peanuts.

In a medium bowl, combine the cheese, pimientos, mayonnaise, Worcestershire sauce, Tabasco, granulated onion, granulated garlic, mustard, paprika, white pepper, and sugar. Using your hands, mix thoroughly until creamy. Season with salt to taste. Refrigerate for 4 hours before serving.

The pimento cheese will keep in an airtight container in the refrigerator for 7 days.

Tex-Mex PIMENTO CHEESE

MAKES 4 CUPS

While working at Oxford's Downtown Grille in the 1990s, when guacamole was all the rage, Dixie invented this now-famous recipe. She tweaked the traditional concept by substituting pepper jack cheese, a little sour cream, and a dose of jalapeños. It sells like hotcakes and pairs well with bacon for a simple sandwich. We also have a crazy good sandwich on the menu that piles this pimento cheese, Dixie's Grilled Chicken Breasts (page 51), Sriracha Coleslaw (page 119), and chopped bread-and-butter pickles on a ciabatta roll. Phew, boy, is it good!

In a medium bowl, combine the cheese, pimientos, jalapeños, mayonnaise, sour cream, lime juice, granulated garlic, granulated onion, cumin, chili powder, and sugar. Season to taste with salt and pepper. Using your hands, mix thoroughly until creamy. Refrigerate for 4 hours before serving.

The pimento cheese will keep in an airtight container in the refrigerator for 7 days.

1 pound pepper jack cheese, shredded (4 cups)

¼ cup chopped pimientos

¼ cup chopped jalapeño peppers

½ cup Hellmann's mayonnaise

¼ cup sour cream

1 tablespoon fresh lime juice

1 teaspoon granulated garlic

1 teaspoon granulated onion

¼ teaspoon ground cumin

¼ teaspoon chili powder

Pinch of sugar

Salt and freshly ground black pepper

HAM *and* HORSERADISH SPREAD

MAKES 4 CUPS

2 cups chopped smoked ham

4 green onions, chopped

1 (4-ounce) jar chopped pimientos, drained

2 tablespoons chopped black olives

1 cup Hellmann's mayonnaise

½ cup sour cream

¼ cup sweet pickle relish

¼ cup prepared horseradish

2 tablespoons fresh lemon juice

1 tablespoon dry white wine

1 tablespoon Worcestershire sauce

1 teaspoon Dijon mustard

1 teaspoon dry mustard

½ teaspoon sugar

½ teaspoon freshly ground black pepper

Crackers, for serving

Something about the word *spread* makes me think of the Depression and old white women with fancy china.

"Back in the day," Dixie says, "if you had yourself a spread and some lettuce leaves, it looked like you really had something."

It took me a while to move beyond the imagined taste of old perfume that rises in my throat at the whole idea of spreads and actually try the stuff, but boy, those elderly ladies are onto something.

For one, spreads are made for entertaining. You can easily swipe a cracker with some and keep on talking. You don't have to worry about something oozing out the back end and sabotaging your Sunday best. And if you're the one hosting a tailgate event, a backyard party, or any kind of social event where you're not sitting at a table, you'll find it's so much easier to set up a crystal cake platter ringed with Carr's crackers and cherry tomatoes with a mound of spread in the center, sprinkled with sweet paprika for color, than to stuff egg rolls or endure Costco for those flaky spinach things everybody always has.

Ham and horseradish also makes a great sandwich. It's good on croissants, mini cocktail breads for a party, or on just-toasted what-have-you for an everyday lunch.

In a food processor, combine the ham and onions. Pulse until finely chopped. Transfer to a bowl and add the pimientos, olives, mayonnaise, sour cream, relish, horseradish, lemon juice, wine, Worcestershire sauce, Dijon mustard, dry mustard, sugar, and pepper. Chill in the refrigerator for 24 hours.

Put the spread in a serving bowl, and serve with crackers on the side.

The King and Queen of Water Valley

SNOOKY AND MARY LOU WILLIAMS are beloved characters around here.

Married for over fifty years, Snooky and Mary Lou moved to Water Valley a heck of a long time ago. Snooky hails from Philadelphia, Mississippi, and is a member of the Williams family, a tight-knit clan famous (or notorious, depending who you ask) for their old country store and the parties they throw at the Neshoba County Fair. Mary Lou is a city girl from Texas. Before she met Snooky, she had married a promising young architect who died swiftly and tragically from cancer, leaving her a widow in her twenties with two young children. She met Snooky a few years later, and he adopted her children and raised them as his own, along with a son that they had together.

I think the reason everybody loves Snooky and Mary Lou is because they so clearly enjoy themselves. If you're with them, it is going to be a big time, no two ways about it. Everything—from hummingbirds to riding around downtown in their new golf cart to loading up their SUV with other senior citizens to go eat tamales and drink beer in the Delta—is cause for celebration.

I was a timid young thing in a rented house with a husband who was at work all day and no friends, no family, and no job. These two took me under their wing and introduced Kagan and me to everyone they knew— which is everyone. They picked me up on Thursday afternoons to drive up to Oxford where Kagan would join us at Off Square Books to watch the Thacker Mountain Radio Show (a world-class weekly entertainment show featuring excellent music, writing, and other acts, and absolutely 100 percent free to attend). Mary Lou invited me to the Friday morning Literary Club down the street at Turnage Drug Store. Book discussion is brief, laughter levels are high, and nothing—and I mean nothing—is off-limits. It was incredibly relaxing to sit among those ladies and let the words wash over me—even more so when Annaliese was born and there were twenty other people thrilled to hold the baby while I drank a cup of coffee and engaged in adult conversation.

Snooky and Mary Lou have lived in Water Valley for a half century and enjoyed all their meals during that time, thank you very much. They weren't holding their breath waiting for the B.T.C. to open, which makes every purchase of theirs all the more meaningful. Last summer, as they prepared for the Neshoba County Fair (which involves feeding scores of people for a week), Mary Lou sent Snooky down to bring her home a sample of our pimento cheese. We waited with bated breath. Sure enough, it passed the test, and she returned Snooky to us bearing her own Tupperware container, which we happily filled. Mary Lou ended up feeding our pimento cheese to a *New York Times* reporter who deemed it merited a mention in the world's greatest paper (although she assumed Mary Lou had made it!).

Even though it's been a while since I rode out on an adventure with the Williamses, I know I always can if the spirit moves me. They are good folks—the best folks—and when newcomers come to town and look like scared deer in headlights, I make sure they find Snooky and Mary Lou. Because they'll be in very good hands.

CLASSIC COLESLAW

SERVES 4

½ medium head white cabbage, quartered

1 small green bell pepper, cut in half, cored, and seeded

1 medium carrot

1 kosher pickle

2 tablespoons sweet pickle relish

1 tablespoon finely chopped yellow onion

1 tablespoon sugar

⅓ cup Hellmann's mayonnaise

2 tablespoons apple cider vinegar (Dixie prefers the Bragg brand)

1 teaspoon yellow mustard

Dash of Tabasco sauce

½ teaspoon garlic powder

⅛ teaspoon celery seeds

⅛ teaspoon chopped fresh dill

Salt and freshly ground black pepper

I am going to admit that growing up, coleslaw did nothing for me. My mother, ever the mayonnaise fiend (she has been known to make mayo sandwiches), adores it and orders it everywhere. But I never saw the appeal—until I came to Mississippi.

Turns out coleslaw tastes best on a pulled pork sandwich, preferably from D&D's House of BBQ. Coleslaw on a BBQ sandwich is something common in Mississippi. Its creamy crunch is just perfect with tender pulled pork smothered in tangy tomato-based sauce (as we do it here).

Of course, you can just eat it as a side too, with Mustard Dill Potato Salad (page 93) or with some Skillet Biscuits (page 18).

In a food processor, combine the cabbage, bell pepper, carrot, and pickle and pulse until finely chopped. Transfer the vegetables to a large glass bowl and add 3 tablespoons of water and the relish, onion, sugar, mayonnaise, vinegar, mustard, Tabasco, garlic powder, celery seeds, and dill. Season with salt and pepper to taste and stir well. The salad can be served immediately, but it's best if you let it sit in the refrigerator overnight. Serve cold or room temperature.

The salad will keep in an airtight container in the refrigerator for 5 days.

SRIRACHA COLESLAW

SERVES 4

The last time Dixie made this, our good friend and great customer Coulter texted both of us on Friday evening. "Eating D&D's ribs with your Sriracha coleslaw," she wrote. "May die of happiness."

D&D's House of BBQ is a fellow new business on Water Valley's Main Street. Prior to launching a brick-and-mortar location, the owner, DeMarq, sold BBQ on the weekends out of a food trailer parked across from the Piggly Wiggly. DeMarq is a hardworking, baby-faced sweetheart who comes to eat breakfast with us regularly, always ordering the exact same plate of scrambled eggs with hoop cheese, which is now known as a "DeMarq." (It's not on the menu; half the menu isn't on the menu.)

His coleslaw is very good, but it is not like the Sriracha coleslaw: crunchy with a kick. We pair ours in-house with Tex-Mex Pimento Cheese (page 115) and Dixie's Grilled Chicken Breasts (page 51) on a ciabatta roll with bread-and-butter pickles—a sandwich known as the "Say Dixie." And of course, it's good enough to eat on its own.

1 head green cabbage, shredded

3 medium carrots, grated (1½ cups)

1 small green bell pepper, cored, seeded, and grated

½ cup dill pickle relish

1 cup Hellmann's mayonnaise

¼ cup Sriracha chili sauce

2 tablespoons apple cider vinegar (Dixie prefers the Bragg brand)

1 teaspoon yellow mustard

¼ cup sugar

1 teaspoon celery seeds

1 teaspoon salt

½ teaspoon freshly ground black pepper

Put the cabbage, carrots, bell pepper, relish, mayonnaise, Sriracha, vinegar, mustard, sugar, celery seeds, salt, pepper, and 1 teaspoon of water in a large bowl. Using your hands, mix the ingredients until well combined. Chill in the refrigerator overnight.

Serve cold. The coleslaw will keep in an airtight container in the refrigerator for 5 days.

RED CABBAGE COLESLAW *with* GOLDEN RAISINS

SERVES 4

Kagan, the aforementioned chain-saw-wielding Yankee husband, is a Renaissance man. He was one of those obnoxious guys during wedding planning who had actual opinions about our big day. He weed-whacks and renovates and changes the oil in our vehicles, sure, but he also does the lion's share of cooking in our household on traditional feast days, like Thanksgiving and Christmas, and thus he sets the menu. We always have ham. He loves, loves, loves ham.

So last Easter, I told him in no uncertain words that this was going to be *my* holiday to plan and execute. I paged through luscious food magazines and harassed Dixie and she gave me this recipe for red cabbage coleslaw.

I won't lie. My children wouldn't eat it. But Kagan and I were wowed by both the taste (sweet and herbed and a light complement to a holiday dinner) and the look (beautiful way to add vibrant color) of this coleslaw.

It theoretically could go well with ham.

TARRAGON VINAIGRETTE

¼ cup extra-virgin olive oil

½ cup tarragon vinegar or apple cider vinegar (Dixie prefers the Bragg brand)

1 tablespoon honey

1 teaspoon dry white wine

1 teaspoon Dijon mustard

1 teaspoon finely chopped shallot

2 teaspoons chopped fresh tarragon

1 teaspoon salt

½ teaspoon freshly ground black pepper

SALAD

1 head purple cabbage, shredded

1 cup golden raisins

1 teaspoon caraway seeds

For the vinaigrette, put the oil, vinegar, honey, wine, mustard, shallots, tarragon, salt, and pepper in a blender and blend for 1 minute. The vinaigrette will keep in an airtight container in the refrigerator for 5 days.

For the salad, in a large bowl, combine the cabbage, raisins, caraway seeds. Pour the vinaigrette over the mixture and toss to combine. Refrigerate for 24 hours.

Serve cold. The salad will keep in an airtight container in the refrigerator for 4 days.

B.T.C. CRANBERRY SAUCE

MAKES 2 CUPS

This, in my opinion, is the pièce de résistance of the holiday meal. I am already partial to cranberry sauce, but this is hands-down better than I could have ever imagined the stuff could be. As long as Dixie makes it, I will buy it.

She whips up a ton of it to sell in the store, and if there is any left over after Thanksgiving, she uses it on special sandwiches until it's all gone. My particular favorite of said sandwiches is a wrap of this sauce with B.T.C. Tuna Salad (page 98) with spinach. It's also great as a background flavor for a simple deli sandwich or wrap of smoked turkey with fresh vegetables of your choice.

1 (12-ounce) bag fresh cranberries

¼ cup cranberry juice (do not use cranberry cocktail)

1 cup sugar

1 cinnamon stick

1 teaspoon ground cinnamon

Grated zest of 1 orange

In a deep pot set over low heat, combine the cranberries, cranberry juice, sugar, cinnamon stick, ground cinnamon, and orange zest. Cook for 1 hour, stirring constantly.

Eventually, the cranberries will start to pop open and their natural pectin will start to thicken the sauce.

Remove the pot from the heat and let cool. Transfer to an airtight container and refrigerate for 24 hours before serving.

Serve cold. The cranberry sauce will keep in the refrigerator for up to 6 days.

FANCY MAYO

There are days in the B.T.C. when the bell on the door seldom tinkles. When the compressors whir, keeping untouched bottles of milk and lonely forlorn vegetables chilled; when fresh bread cools unnoticed and fried pies settle to room temperature and the cash register never hits its jangling stride.

Days like that used to break my heart. I'm thin-skinned, always have been, and on slow days when the only thing anybody wanted from me was a single tomato, I'd trudge home. Be really snappy with my husband until the truth came welling out: I am failing. I have failed. It is over, we are done, I don't see a way out of this mess. It's too small of a town. We're too different. Folks like Wal-Mart too much. (See, when you don't make any money, the day, very sadly, does not cost any less: payroll still has to be made, the utility bill still has to be paid.)

We are pretty firmly grounded these days, although like most small brick-and-mortar businesses, it's still touch-and-go financially. But the difference is we've got an established customer base, so the wild highs and lows of the first eighteen months have steadied a bit.

That being said, we still have those days.

Two this week, in fact.

I don't panic as much as I used to, but I do still wonder about the probability of clawing out a living in a town of thirty-five hundred in a poor state in a depressed economy. Most days, I think, Sure! A couple more years and we'll get to the point where Dixie and I will make something approaching a Mississippi-level decent living.

But on days when the air is still and the store is empty, I think about our ace in the hole.

Mayonnaise. Flavored mayonnaises, to be precise.

Dixie makes an assortment of these at the store for various sandwiches. The caramelized red onion and cranberry goes on our roast beef sandwich, known as "Wagner's Revenge," and it's a best seller: roast beef, Muenster cheese, arugula, and the fancy mayo all on a ciabatta roll rolled in sea salt and caraway seeds.

Sometimes people order a "Wagner's Revenge" without the mayo. It's a minor tragedy.

These mayonnaises are so good, I think we should bottle and sell 'em and get them on every mainstream supermarket shelf in the nation, and then Dixie and I wouldn't have to worry about people coming through the door of 301 North Main.

CHERRY MAYONNAISE

1 cup Hellmann's mayonnaise

1 tablespoon fresh lime juice

½ cup cherry preserves

⅛ cup chopped dried cherries

⅛ teaspoon ground allspice

Dash of crushed red pepper flakes

Salt

MAKES ABOUT 1 CUP

In a medium bowl, combine the mayonnaise, lime juice, preserves, dried cherries, allspice, and pepper flakes. Season to taste with salt. Refrigerate for 24 hours before serving.

The mayonnaise will keep in an airtight container in the refrigerator for 2 weeks.

TOMATO CAPER MAYONNAISE

1 cup Hellmann's mayonnaise

1 teaspoon Worcestershire sauce

1 teaspoon fresh lemon juice

¼ cup capers

½ small tomato, cored, seeded, and chopped (¼ cup)

1 tablespoon granulated garlic

1 tablespoon granulated onion

½ teaspoon white pepper

½ teaspoon kosher salt

MAKES ABOUT 1 CUP

In a bowl, whisk together the mayonnaise, Worcestershire sauce, lemon juice, capers, tomatoes, granulated garlic, granulated onion, white pepper, and salt. Refrigerate for 4 hours before serving.

The mayonnaise will keep in an airtight container in the refrigerator for 2 weeks.

Dixie and Annaliese's
ROASTED RED PEPPER SALSA

SERVES 4

Lately, Dixie has been jonesing for a kitchen assistant. Monday through Friday, Dixie makes every salad, spread, casserole, and soup in the store, in between flipping eggs for all our breakfast customers and making sandwiches for our lunches. She is a one-woman whirling dervish in the kitchen, and lately she's been hinting she'd like some help.

I like to respond to my employees' requests, so I have started bringing in my five-year-old daughter even more regularly than before. Annaliese loves the kitchen, working alongside Dixie, standing on a cooler at a stainless-steel table chopping artichoke hearts or adding olives to a platter of salad or stirring up a giant bowl of roasted red pepper salsa with a whisk as big as she is.

Dixie and Annaliese are kindred spirits: Something in one recognizes something in the other. They were both born on January 6, the day of Epiphany, and both can be obstinate, moody, and difficult. They comprehend each other in a way my sunny Libra self can't, and so it's easy for me to step out of the kitchen, restock the apples, and let the two of them get onto the business of making stuff back in the kitchen.

They make this salsa together often. It's a smoother salsa with a great flavor, perfect for folks of any age.

2 cups tomato sauce

1 (16-ounce) jar roasted red peppers, drained and pureed

1 tablespoon fresh lime juice

1 tablespoon red wine vinegar

4 dashes Tabasco sauce

1 tablespoon chopped fresh parsley

1 tablespoon chopped fresh cilantro

1 tablespoon ground cumin

1 tablespoon chili powder

1 tablespoon ground coriander

1 teaspoon granulated garlic

1 teaspoon granulated onion

½ teaspoon sugar

½ teaspoon freshly ground black pepper

Salt

Tortilla chips, for serving

In a large bowl, whisk together the tomato sauce, red pepper puree, lime juice, vinegar, Tabasco, parsley, cilantro, cumin, chili powder, coriander, granulated garlic, granulated onion, sugar, and pepper. Season with salt to taste. Cover the bowl with plastic wrap and chill in the refrigerator overnight.

Serve with tortilla chips. The salsa will keep in an airtight container in the refrigerator for 5 days.

Want to Be a Better Person? Start a Small Business.

BEFORE I OPENED the grocery store, I drove over to see Frank, the owner and operator at Stan's Meats outside of Oxford, an excellent store that cures their own salamis and cuts grass-fed steaks to order. I sat down with Frank and asked him what to expect running a small food business.

He took a deep drag of a cigarette and told me the truth: It would be hard. Expensive. That maybe 10 percent of my customers on opening day would ever come back, and once I had that 10 percent, I was going to have to work hard to find the items they wanted to buy.

I drove away from that talk thinking that Frank was raining on my parade. It couldn't be that hard, I thought. Slap some price tags on the kind of foods I like, put it on the shelves, and open the doors. That was my informal business plan.

I've been an idiot before in my life.

He was completely, totally, irrevocably correct.

A year into running the store, plagued by bills and depressing totals, I'd developed a horrendous habit: constantly tallying the friends and neighbors who did shop with me versus the ones who did not. For instance, John Crow, a lawyer with an office located in sight of the B.T.C.'s back door, never stopped by for a sandwich, a soda, an apple, anything.

It rankled. I let it rankle me. I hadn't learned to be patient yet. Hadn't realized yet that maybe the fault wasn't with the customer but with my store. Maybe we needed to do a better job of identifying and filling our customers' needs rather than presuming on their goodwill.

Thirteen months after we'd opened, Mr. Crow came in. He ordered the classic: smoked turkey, dill Havarti, lettuce, tomato, mayonnaise, mustard, on freshly baked sourdough bread. He ate thoroughly and alone, and the look on his face tickled me, because it looked like disturbed surprise. The next few times he came in, it was the same order, same expression.

About the fourth time he ordered that sandwich, I stopped by to chat.

"How is everything?" I asked.

"Good?" he said. He said the word like he was still shocked that the first three sandwiches weren't flukes and this one was tasty, too.

"How come you sound so surprised?" I asked.

Mr. Crow snorted and shook his head. "I just never thought I'd eat this kind of sandwich in Water Valley."

I never thought Frank at Stan's Meats would be right, either. Color us both surprised.

GREEN OLIVE TAPENADE

SERVES 4

Whenever I tell folks about why I started the B.T.C., olives enter the story. The short version goes like this: Water Valley had just about everything I needed, except a place to buy the kind of food I like to eat. There is a Piggly Wiggly, a successful grocery store that has served Water Valley for decades and will continue to do so, but they lacked a couple of things that I find important. As in, they carry pigs' feet and cans of calf brains in milk gravy, but there are no good olives to be had.

Cerignola olives are very, very good. Large, green, and from the town of Cerignola in the Italian province of Foggia, they have a pleasing, succulent, and mild flavor without any bitterness. Consequently, this tapenade winds up as flavorful and savory. It's perfect for sandwiches, brushing on chicken breasts, smearing on top of an omelet or frittata, or eating with crackers and good cheese.

1 pound green Cerignola olives, pitted

4 anchovy fillets

6 tablespoons capers

3 garlic cloves

6 tablespoons extra-virgin olive oil

Juice of ½ lemon

Pinch of crushed red pepper flakes

Note
For black olive tapenade, substitute Kalamata olives for the Cerignola.

In a food processor, combine the olives, anchovies, capers, garlic, oil, lemon juice, and red pepper flakes. Pulse until the mixture is smooth, scraping down the sides of the bowl as necessary.

Serve at room temperature. The tapenade will keep in an airtight container in the refrigerator for 5 days.

BUTTERMILK RANCH DRESSING

1 cup Hellmann's mayonnaise

½ cup buttermilk

1 tablespoon fresh lemon juice

1 teaspoon Worcestershire sauce

Dash of Tabasco sauce

1 teaspoon granulated garlic

1 teaspoon onion powder

1 teaspoon granulated onion

1 teaspoon dry mustard

1 teaspoon sweet paprika

1 teaspoon sugar

1 tablespoon dried dill weed

1 tablespoon dried parsley

1 teaspoon freshly ground black pepper

Salt

Of all the salad dressings the B.T.C. now makes, buttermilk ranch is the one I snubbed when I moved to the Deep South. People down here stick their wings, cut-up vegetables, and potato chips in it, as well as drenching salads with it. I turned my nose up.

But, y'all, it's delicious, and my Yankee husband thinks so, too. A certain German PhD here in town has declared she could drink it. We sell chopped salads that are a perfect excuse for eating it. I justify my weekly purchase of a bottle from the B.T.C. cooler like this: It's fresh, no preservatives or anything like that, and when I stick a piece of broccoli or raw spinach into it, my kids will eat it.

Plus, you can dip chips into it.

In a medium bowl, whisk together the mayonnaise, buttermilk, lemon juice, Worcestershire sauce, Tabasco, granulated garlic, onion powder, granulated onion, mustard, paprika, sugar, dill, parsley, and pepper until smooth. Season to taste with salt. You can serve it immediately, though it's best if it's refrigerated overnight.

The dressing will keep in an airtight container in the refrigerator for 2 weeks.

Thousand Island
DRESSING

MAKES 3 CUPS

Oxford, the home of Ole Miss and the cultural mecca of Mississippi, has become controversial in the way of many small towns that enjoy high rates of tourism and university salaries.

But one vestige of "old Oxford" remains, and it is aptly named the Beacon. The Beacon is a greasy spoon famous for many things, and one of them is a salad that consists of a head of iceberg lettuce cut in half, dropped in a bowl with two wedges of tomato and two slices of cucumber, and anointed with Thousand Island dressing.

Obviously, the secret is in the dressing. It's great on salads of all ambition levels.

1 cup **Hellmann's mayonnaise**

1 cup **Heinz chili sauce**

¼ cup **tomato sauce**

½ cup **ketchup**

3 tablespoons **Worcestershire sauce**

1 **hard-boiled egg, grated**

¼ cup **grated sweet pickles**

2 tablespoons **grated dill pickles**

1 teaspoon **white pepper**

Dash of Tabasco sauce

In a large bowl, combine the mayonnaise, chili sauce, tomato sauce, ketchup, Worcestershire sauce, egg, sweet and dill pickles, white pepper, and Tabasco. Cover the bowl and refrigerate overnight.

Serve cold. The dressing will keep in an airtight container in the refrigerator for 7 days.

KAGAN'S DILL PICKLES

MAKES 8 QUART JARS

8 pounds (3- to 4-inch-long) pickling cucumbers (Kagan slices his; Dan pickles his whole)

4 cups white vinegar

⅔ cup kosher salt

16 garlic cloves, peeled and halved

16 large sprigs fresh dill

A couple of years ago, I was browsing the nation's finest bookstore (not joking; it's awesome), Square Books in Oxford, Mississippi, and I found a book called *Man with a Pan*. It included essays by fathers about cooking for their families, with recipes included.

At the time, Kagan and I were in transition mode. I'd been at home for several years, and he'd worked full-time. The "what's for dinner" dilemma had been all mine, at least on the weekdays. But now I had a job. We were both coming home from work, everybody was hungry, and I needed him to think beyond opening a can or dumping frozen veggies in a pot, because frankly I wanted him to make me something tasty on the nights it was his turn.

So I bought the book.

I read it. He read it. He tried some recipes. But out of all the recipes, the one he is still making is a pickle recipe from Dan Moulthrop, who himself got the recipe off the Internet from a woman named Sharon.

Kagan's family adores pickles. He grew up eating pickled watermelon rind, pears, peaches, asparagus, green beans—you name it. Just about everything can be put in a jar full of vinegar if you're a Coughlin.

Me? I'm not such a mad lover of pickles. Dixie and Annaliese are, though, so every summer I get ahold of some pickling cucumbers—short and straight—for Kagan, and he spends an afternoon filling quart jars. Dixie swears these are the best she's ever had: crisp and full of flavor.

Pickles. It's what's for dinner.

Put the cucumbers in a large bowl and cover them with cold water and lots of ice. Let soak for no less than 2 hours and no more than 8. This is a crucial step, so don't skip it. Refresh the ice as needed.

Meanwhile, sterilize eight 1-quart canning jars and lids by submerging them in boiling water for at least 10 minutes.

In a large pot set over medium-high heat, combine 12 cups of water with the vinegar and salt. Bring the brine to a rapid boil.

In each sterilized jar, put 2 pieces of garlic and 1 dill sprig, and then pack tightly with cucumbers. Add 2 more pieces of garlic and 1 more dill sprig. Fill the jars to the top with hot brine. Screw the lids onto the jars, making sure to clean up any spills. Process the jars in a boiling water bath for 15 minutes. Remove the jars and let them cool completely.

Store the pickles for at least 8 weeks before eating. Refrigerate after opening. If kept in a cool dark place, the pickles will keep, unopened, for up to 2 years.

Casseroles

SOUTHERN YELLOW SQUASH CASSEROLE

CORN BREAD SQUASH CASSEROLE

GREEN APPLE CASSEROLE

BAKED BRUSSELS SPROUTS CASSEROLE

ARTICHOKE *and* ENGLISH PEA AU GRATIN

HOOP *and* HAVARTI MACARONI

DIXIE'S SWEET POTATO CASSEROLE *with*
MARSHMALLOWS *and* COCONUT CRUMBLE

SWEET POTATO *and* GREEN CHILE CASSEROLE

CHICKEN SPAGHETTI

CHICKEN 'N' DUMPLINGS

CHICKEN POT PIE *with* PARSNIPS
and ROASTED LEEKS

CHICKEN, ASPARAGUS,
and MUSHROOM CASSEROLE

OYSTER CASSEROLE

SOUTHWESTERN BEEF CASSEROLE

DIXIE'S LASAGNA

SOUTHERN YELLOW SQUASH CASSEROLE

SERVES 4

Sweet, savory, with crunchy bits, this casserole works well for everything from weekday suppers to holiday dinners.

Preheat the oven to 350°F. Spray a 9 × 13-inch casserole dish with nonstick cooking spray.

In an 8-quart stockpot set over medium heat, combine the squash, onion, and bell pepper. Cover with water, bring to a boil, and cook until the squash is just soft, 10 minutes. Drain the mixture, discarding the liquid, and return to the pot. Add the cheeses, pimientos, eggs, mayonnaise, vermouth, Worcestershire sauce, Tabasco, basil, granulated onion, granulated garlic, and sugar. Season with salt and pepper. Mix well, scoop into the prepared casserole dish, and sprinkle the bread crumbs over the top.

Bake until golden brown, 30 to 45 minutes.

Note
This casserole will keep in the freezer for up to 3 months. For best results, freeze it before baking; thaw overnight in the refrigerator, and then bake according to the recipe.

2 pounds yellow squash, chopped

1 medium yellow onion, finely chopped (1½ cups)

2 tablespoons chopped green bell pepper

¼ pound Cheddar cheese, shredded (1 cup)

¼ pound pepper jack cheese, shredded (1 cup)

1 (4-ounce) jar diced pimientos, drained

2 eggs, beaten

⅓ cup Hellmann's mayonnaise

1 tablespoon dry vermouth

1 teaspoon Worcestershire sauce

Dash of Tabasco sauce

1 teaspoon dried basil

1 teaspoon granulated onion

1 teaspoon granulated garlic

⅛ teaspoon sugar

Salt and freshly ground black pepper

1½ cup panko bread crumbs

CORN BREAD
SQUASH *Casserole*

SERVES 4

If you're fond of corn bread and cheese, this is your lucky day. This casserole combines fresh squash and zucchini with crumbled corn bread and slathers it in cheese for a side that Southerners eat year-round.

¼ cup (½ stick) unsalted butter

1 medium yellow onion, finely chopped (1½ cups)

2 tablespoons finely chopped green bell pepper

½ pound yellow squash, thinly sliced (2 cups)

½ pound zucchini, thinly sliced (2 cups)

3 cups crumbled Dixie's Corn Bread (page 197)

¾ pound Cheddar cheese, shredded (3 cups)

⅓ cup heavy cream

⅓ cup Chicken Stock, homemade (page 45) or store-bought

1 tablespoon chopped fresh parsley

1 tablespoon chopped fresh rosemary

1 teaspoon chopped fresh thyme

1 tablespoon granulated garlic

1 teaspoon dried sage

1 teaspoon freshly ground black pepper

2 eggs, beaten

Preheat the oven to 350°F. Spray a 9 × 13-inch casserole dish with nonstick cooking spray.

In a sauté pan set over medium heat, melt the butter. Add the onion and bell pepper and cook, stirring, until soft, 12 minutes. Add the squash and zucchini and cook, stirring, until the squash is soft, 10 minutes. Pour the vegetables into a large bowl and add the corn bread, 1½ cups of the cheese, the cream, stock, parsley, rosemary, thyme, granulated garlic, sage, and pepper. Add the eggs and stir until thoroughly combined.

Pour the mixture into the prepared casserole dish. Sprinkle the remaining cheese over the top. Bake until the cheese is melted and bubbly, 30 to 40 minutes. Serve hot.

Note
This casserole will keep in the freezer for up to 3 months. For best results, freeze it before baking; thaw overnight in the refrigerator, and then bake according to the recipe.

GREEN APPLE CASSEROLE

SERVES 4

This casserole is solely Dixie's creation. It came about from something you occasionally see happening in diners: old folks asking for a slice of cheese on top of their apple pie. It doesn't sound good, but it works.

And so does this casserole. Dixie likes to serve it for spring and fall bridal showers or other occasions where pretty-looking and good-tasting food is called for. It's especially pretty if you cook it in individual ramekins.

- ¼ cup (½ stick) unsalted butter, plus more for the dish
- 3 pounds Granny Smith apples, peeled, cored, and sliced
- 2 tablespoons applejack or apple brandy
- 1 teaspoon fresh lemon juice
- ¾ cup packed light brown sugar
- ⅓ cup all-purpose flour
- ½ teaspoon ground cinnamon
- ¼ pound extra-sharp Cheddar cheese, shredded (a heaping ½ cup)

Preheat the oven to 300°F. Grease an 8 × 8-inch baking dish or 4 individual ramekins with butter.

In a large bowl, combine the apples, applejack, and lemon juice.

In a separate bowl, combine the sugar, flour, and cinnamon. Cut in the butter until the mixture resembles small peas, and then add the cheese. In the bottom of the prepared dish, make a layer of half of the apples, and then sprinkle half of the dry ingredients in a second layer; repeat the layers with the remaining ingredients.

Bake until the cheese is melted and bubbly, 40 minutes (25 minutes for ramekins).

Note

This casserole will keep in the freezer for up to 3 months. For best results, freeze it before baking; thaw overnight in the refrigerator, and then bake according to the recipe.

BAKED BRUSSELS SPROUTS *Casserole*

SERVES 4 TO 6

This casserole is dense, rich, hearty, and as decadent as a casserole involving small green cabbages can be. It's a very good tool for soothing the soul and uplifting the spirits on a cold winter night.

Preheat the oven to 375°F. Spray a 9 × 13-inch skillet with nonstick cooking spray.

In a large sauté pan set over medium heat, heat 2 tablespoons of the oil. Add the prosciutto, shallots, and garlic and cook, stirring, until the shallots are soft, about 10 minutes. Add the Brussels sprouts and cook until tender, 15 minutes. Transfer the mixture to a bowl and set aside.

Add the remaining 2 tablespoons oil to the pan. Add the flour and cook, stirring constantly, until smooth and creamy, 3 to 5 minutes. Whisk in the cream, stock, sherry, and vinegar. Bring the mixture to a simmer, and add both cheeses, the nutmeg, white pepper, and pepper flakes. Season with salt to taste. Stir until the cheese melts, turn off the heat, and stir in the Brussels sprouts mixture. Scoop the mixture into the prepared skillet and sprinkle the bread crumbs over the top.

Bake until the top is golden brown, about 45 minutes.

4 tablespoons extra-virgin olive oil

8 slices (¼ pound) prosciutto, chopped

2 shallots, finely chopped

2 garlic cloves, minced

2 pounds Brussels sprouts, quartered

2 tablespoons all-purpose flour

2 cups heavy cream

¼ cup Chicken Stock, homemade (page 45) or store-bought

2 tablespoons sherry (Dixie prefers Harveys Bristol Cream)

1 tablespoon red wine vinegar

½ cup grated aged Asiago cheese

2 ounces Swiss cheese, shredded (½ cup)

⅛ teaspoon ground nutmeg

⅛ teaspoon white pepper

Dash of crushed red pepper flakes

Salt

2 cups panko bread crumbs

Note

This casserole will keep in the freezer for up to 3 months. For best results, freeze it before baking; thaw overnight in the refrigerator, and then bake according to the recipe.

ARTICHOKE *and* ENGLISH PEA
Au Gratin

8 cups frozen English peas, thawed but not cooked

2 cups frozen artichoke hearts, thawed and quartered

2 cups heavy cream

1 tablespoon Worcestershire sauce

1 tablespoon dry white wine

2 cups shredded Parmesan cheese

1 garlic clove, minced

1 teaspoon dried basil

1 teaspoon freshly ground black pepper

½ teaspoon ground nutmeg

½ teaspoon kosher salt

1 cup panko bread crumbs

Note
This casserole will keep in the freezer for up to 3 months. For best results, freeze it before baking; thaw overnight in the refrigerator, and then bake according to the recipe.

This casserole contains all the comfort of macaroni and cheese but with an adult twist. It's not actually my favorite way to eat artichokes (I prefer to eat them steamed with a ramekin of melted butter), but I can tell you that we keep this casserole in the B.T.C.'s freezer at all times because when we run out, folks fuss.

Preheat the oven to 375°F. Spray a 9 × 9-inch baking dish with nonstick cooking spray.

In a large bowl, combine the peas and artichokes; set aside.

In a separate medium bowl, combine the cream, Worcestershire sauce, wine, cheese, garlic, basil, pepper, nutmeg, and salt. Gently fold the cream mixture into the peas and artichokes. Pour the mixture into the prepared baking dish and sprinkle the bread crumbs on the top.

Bake until the casserole is bubbly and the bread crumbs are golden brown, 45 minutes. Let sit for 15 minutes before serving.

Billy Ray Brown

BILLY RAY BROWN is the fellow who brings me ice-cold glass bottles of milk—fresh milk—from his dairy twice a week. A true-blue country boy, he is funny as hell. And—and this is the part I imagine some folks forget—he's smarter than you and me put together.

Way before Billy Ray ever had a dairy, a lot of people already knew about him. His father, Larry Brown, was an extraordinary man in his own right and a prolific writer. One of Larry's books is a collection of essays called *Billy Ray's Farm,* which details Billy Ray's early years of farming. Billy Ray has been farming something or another since he was in high school; it is, quite simply, all he ever wanted to do. So he has been raising beef cattle and pigs and just about everything else on the land he grew up on—a tract of family land outside Oxford in an odd little community called Yocona (pronounced "Yokna").

A few years ago, Billy Ray was in Wal-Mart, and after a conversation with a store manager about where the organic milk came from (Colorado) and how it was selling (flying off the shelves), he decided to open his own microdairy. It took a few years—he built his dairy with his own two hands while doing town maintenance full-time for the City of Oxford. There was also a massive amount of red tape he had to wade through. It'd been years since anybody opened a small, farm-to-consumer, approved-for-retail dairy, and the Mississippi Department of Health inspectors didn't quite know what to do with him.

But Billy Ray got it done, and since he opened, he's been supporting himself and his family (three astoundingly beautiful children and a pretty wife named Paula) off his cows.

Here are some of the things Billy Ray has done or told me since we met:

1. Had a pet goat that lived on the porch with ribbons tied around its horns by the children who thought it was a dog (perhaps because it accompanied Billy Ray on hunting trips).
2. Has spoofed a marketer from AT&T for years now about his life in Mississippi, claiming he can't commit to changing their phone service plan because his wife is in jail after hitting her mama on the head with a skillet after getting into a fight about corn bread, etcetera, etcetera, etcetera.

3. Brought a tiny pet pig named Jimmy Dean on one of his milk deliveries to the B.T.C. As Jimmy Dean pranced on the sidewalk, Billy Ray detailed his nighttime routine of getting up two to four times a night to bottle-feed the tiny pig—though, as he says, he never got up for his own children during their infancies.
4. Discussed literature at great length with me and guilt-tripped me when I told him I had not yet read Michael Pollan's ubiquitous *The Omnivore's Dilemma.*
5. Told me how he and his extended family were drinking beer and hanging out one Friday night when his brother Shane bet a hundred dollars that Billy Ray, no longer the high school athlete, could not run a mile in under ten minutes. Everybody piled in the truck, and Billy Ray set to running, his kids hanging out the windows, screaming, "Go, Daddy, go!" And he went. And he did.

Funny stories aside, Billy Ray's milk is hands-down the best in the world. Ice cold, rich, creamy, and sweet, it is everything milk should be. Indeed, the only complaint I've ever had about it is from someone who declared "it tastes too much like milk." I think that's a good problem to have.

HOOP *and* HAVARTI *Macaroni*

SERVES 4

People in this town have a gift for seeing what needs to be done. When Kagan and I were lost in the throes of new parenthood, our own parents far away, the elders of this town individually stepped toward us with helping hands.

Several days after Annaliese's birth, as Kagan and I stumbled around in our home, trying to orient ourselves around a squalling newborn, someone knocked on the door. I opened it to find Miss Cecil, a majestic and queenly woman with white hair and bright red fingernails. She did not bat an eye at my worn pajama top or stretched-out yoga pants. She sailed into the kitchen, kissed the top of Annaliese's head, and placed a fully roasted turkey on our counter. Then she left. She just figured that we could use a nutritious home-cooked meal, and so she dropped one off.

Life in small towns is not immune to tragedy or plain hard times. But one of the most fundamental ways of helping out is with the gift of food. Macaroni and cheese is one of the foods we all reach for when we want something easy and something good. This particular version is creamy, crunchy, and all things soul-nourishing.

7 tablespoons unsalted butter

1 cup panko bread crumbs

1 tablespoon chopped fresh parsley

2 cups dry elbow macaroni, cooked

¼ cup all-purpose flour

2½ cups heavy cream

1 teaspoon dry mustard

1 teaspoon sweet paprika

1 teaspoon granulated onion

1 teaspoon granulated garlic

1 teaspoon white pepper

⅛ teaspoon ground nutmeg

¼ pound Danish Havarti cheese, shredded (1 cup)

¼ pound red rind hoop cheese, shredded (1 cup)

Note

This casserole will keep in the freezer for up to 3 months. For best results, freeze it before baking; thaw overnight in the refrigerator, and then bake according to the recipe.

Preheat the oven to 350°F. Spray a 9 × 13-inch casserole dish with nonstick cooking spray.

In a small skillet set over medium heat, melt 3 tablespoons of the butter. Add the bread crumbs and parsley. Cook, stirring, until golden brown, 5 minutes. Set aside to let cool.

In a sauté pan set over medium heat, melt the remaining 4 tablespoons butter. Whisk in the flour until smooth and cook, whisking, for 5 minutes. Whisk in the cream, and then add the mustard, paprika, granulated onion, granulated garlic, pepper, and nutmeg. Bring to a simmer. Gradually whisk in both cheeses until melted and fully incorporated. Stir in the cooked macaroni, and pour the mixture into the prepared casserole dish. Top with the bread crumbs.

Bake until the top starts to brown, 30 minutes.

DIXIE'S SWEET POTATO *Casserole with Marshmallows and Coconut Crumble*

This year, I actually ordered a sweet potato casserole from Dixie for Thanksgiving, and while I badly wanted it to come with marshmallows and coconut crumble, it did not. No one received such a casserole, even though it is Dixie's favorite way to make sweet potato casserole. Unfortunately for me, my children sabotaged our holiday operation by opening every single bag of marshmallows in the store, an act discovered at the ninth hour. No one wants a casserole topped with stale, child-fingered marshmallows. So Dixie created an alternative, which was delicious, but it doesn't hold a candle to the original.

Coconut isn't a traditional topping in our neck of the woods by any means, but with the gooey and slightly toasted marshmallows, it's just perfect.

Preheat the oven to 425°F.

For the sweet potatoes, put the potatoes on an ungreased baking sheet and bake until fork-tender, 45 minutes to 1 hour. Let cool, peel, and mash with a fork. You should have about 3 cups.

Reduce the oven temperature to 350°F. Spray an 8 × 8-inch casserole dish with nonstick cooking spray.

In a large bowl, combine the potatoes, evaporated milk, sweetened condensed milk, butter, vanilla, eggs, sugar, cinnamon, allspice, nutmeg, cloves, ginger, and salt. Pour into the prepared casserole dish.

For the crumble, in a medium bowl, combine the sugar, coconut, pecans, flour, and butter until crumbly. Sprinkle the mixture evenly over the sweet potatoes. Top with the marshmallows.

Bake until the marshmallows are golden brown, 30 to 45 minutes.

SWEET POTATOES

1½ pounds sweet potatoes

½ cup evaporated milk

½ cup sweetened condensed milk

¼ cup (½ stick) unsalted butter, melted

1 teaspoon vanilla extract

2 eggs, beaten

½ cup packed light brown sugar

1 tablespoon ground cinnamon

1 teaspoon ground allspice

1 teaspoon ground nutmeg

½ teaspoon ground cloves

½ teaspoon ground ginger

½ teaspoon salt

COCONUT CRUMBLE

1 cup packed light brown sugar

1 cup unsweetened coconut flakes (use fresh, if possible)

1 cup chopped pecans

½ cup all-purpose flour

¼ cup (½ stick) unsalted butter, room temperature

½ (16-ounce) bag marshmallows

SWEET POTATO *and* GREEN CHILE CASSEROLE

SERVES 6

4 pounds sweet potatoes

1 (5-ounce) can chopped mild green chiles

2 tablespoons unsalted butter, melted

1 tablespoon honey

1 tablespoon fresh lime juice

1 egg, beaten

1 teaspoon ground cumin

1 teaspoon chili powder

⅛ teaspoon ground cinnamon

⅛ teaspoon freshly ground black pepper

¼ pound pepper jack cheese, shredded (1 cup)

One of the great ironies of my mother's life is that she is deeply and aspirationally Southern, yet she is also pathologically afraid of sweet potatoes. Hates 'em. Can't serve them if she is at the table, or she gets huffy and nauseated.

So, Mama, this one ain't for you. Which is a shame, because you like a little spice.

For anyone looking to have a lighter and more exotic sweet potato dish year-round or at holiday dinners, this is super savory and healthful as well.

Preheat the oven to 425°F. Spray a 9 × 13-inch baking dish with nonstick cooking spray; set aside.

Put the potatoes on an ungreased baking sheet and bake until fork-tender, 45 minutes to 1 hour. Let cool, peel, and mash with a fork. You should have about 8 cups.

In a large bowl, combine the potatoes, chiles, butter, honey, lime juice, egg, cumin, chili powder, cinnamon, and pepper. Pour into the prepared baking dish and sprinkle the top with the cheese.

Bake until the top starts to brown, 20 to 25 minutes.

CHICKEN SPAGHETTI

SERVES 6

I didn't grow up eating chicken spaghetti, which is a common dish that many of my elderly customers seem know and love. When I first heard of the dish, I pictured it as traditional spaghetti, maybe with shredded chicken unobtrusively hiding in the tomato sauce. Then I went to a restaurant and watched someone order and eat what looked like a beige pile of gluey noodles. I swore to myself that that particular Southern classic would never cross my lips.

I bet you know how this story goes. Dixie made it. It had green peas and mushrooms and didn't look beige; it had a really nice creamy sauce. I tasted some. It was delicious.

In my mind, I ate my words. In actuality, I refilled my plate.

Preheat the oven to 375°F. Spray a 9 × 13-inch casserole dish with nonstick cooking spray.

In a large bowl, combine the cheese, tomatoes, peas, mushrooms, all three soups, egg, and Tabasco. Stir in the chicken and spaghetti. (Dixie prefers to do this by hand to make sure the spaghetti gets well coated.) Pour into the prepared casserole dish.

Bake until the top browns and is bubbly, 30 to 40 minutes. Let sit for 20 minutes before serving.

¼ pound hoop cheese, shredded (1 cup)

1 (10-ounce) can mild Ro-Tel tomatoes

1 (14.5-ounce) can baby peas, drained (Dixie prefers LeSueur brand)

1 (10-ounce) can sliced mushrooms, drained

1 (10-ounce) can Campbell's cream of chicken soup

1 (10-ounce) can Campbell's cream of broccoli soup

1 (10-ounce) can Campbell's Cheddar cheese soup

1 egg, beaten

4 dashes Tabasco sauce

4 cups shredded meat from 1 Boiled Chicken (page 45)

1 (16-ounce) package thin spaghetti, cooked and drained

Note

This casserole will keep in the freezer for up to 3 months. For best results, freeze it before baking; thaw overnight in the refrigerator, and then bake according to the recipe.

CHICKEN 'N' DUMPLINGS

SERVES 6 TO 8

1½ cups sifted all-purpose flour

3 teaspoons salt

¼ teaspoon baking soda

¼ cup (½ stick) unsalted butter, cold and cut into cubes

4 teaspoons lard

1 egg, beaten

2 cups whole milk

1 (3-pound) fryer chicken, cut into pieces

1 large onion, quartered

1 large carrot, cut in half

2 celery hearts, chopped

4 whole black peppercorns

3 dashes Tabasco sauce

1 tablespoon granulated onion

1 tablespoon granulated garlic

½ teaspoon freshly ground black pepper

⅛ teaspoon white pepper

Pinch of sugar

1½ cups heavy cream

Note
This dish will keep for 3 days in the refrigerator. It does not freeze well.

Chicken and dumplings is one of the greatest soul foods of the South. Dixie learned to make it at her grandmother's knee; one of her first jobs in the kitchen was to make and cut the dumplings. It's the sort of dish you want when you're sick, because, as Dixie says, it will heal you; it will bring you back from the dead. All that being said, it is an all-day pain-in-the-ass recipe to make. So save it for the ones you love.

In a medium bowl, combine the flour, 1 teaspoon of the salt, and the baking soda. Cut in the butter and lard until small pea-size pieces form. Add the egg and ½ cup of the milk. Stir until it forms a ball. Wrap in plastic wrap and refrigerate for at least 30 minutes.

In a stockpot, combine 4 cups of water with the chicken, onion, carrot, celery, peppercorns, and 2 teaspoons of the salt. Bring to a simmer, but do not boil, and cook for 1 hour, until the chicken is tender. Strain the stock into a large bowl and let cool. Let the chicken pieces cool, and then skin and debone them, breaking the meat into bite-size pieces; set aside. Discard the vegetables.

Put the chilled dumpling dough on a well-floured work surface, and using a floured rolling pin, roll out the dough until it is ½ inch thick. Cut it into 2-inch-wide strips and then into bite-size pieces.

Skim the fat off the top of the stock and return the stock to the stockpot over medium-high heat. Bring to a boil and add the remaining 1½ cups milk, Tabasco, granulated onion, granulated garlic, black and white pepper, and sugar. Drop a couple dumplings at a time into the boiling stock. Reduce the heat to medium-low and let simmer, stirring occasionally so that the dumplings do not stick together, until soft, 8 to 10 minutes. Add in the reserved cooked chicken and cook for 20 more minutes. Add the cream and simmer for 10 more minutes. Remove the pot from the heat and let cool for 20 minutes before serving.

CHICKEN POT PIE
with Parsnips and Roasted Leeks

SERVES 6

Pot pies delight the child in all of us. Pie! Full of stuff! And this one is so pretty, with the fresh green peas and golden pastry. It's also grown-up enough, with the parsnips and leeks, to delight the gourmands.

Preheat the oven to 450°F.

Put the leeks on a baking sheet, toss with the oil, and season with salt and pepper. Roast until golden brown, 20 minutes. Set aside to let cool.

Reduce the oven temperature to 400°F.

In a sauté pan set over medium heat, melt ½ cup of the butter. Add the parsnips, carrots, and mushrooms and cook, stirring, until tender, 15 minutes. Add the sherry and cook, stirring, until it has evaporated, 5 minutes. Add the flour and cook, stirring constantly with a wooden spoon, until golden brown and smooth, 5 minutes. Slowly whisk in the stock and heavy cream, and whisk until smooth. Add the chicken, peas, leeks, rosemary, thyme, tarragon, and white pepper. Cook until barely thickened, about 15 minutes. Remove the pan from the heat.

On a floured work surface, roll out the dough to ⅛-inch thickness. Put 1 crust in either an 8 × 8-inch square baking dish or a 9-inch deep-dish pie pan, pressing it against the sides of the dish so that there are no gaps or air bubbles. Pour in the chicken mixture. Put the second pie crust over the top and seal all edges tightly. Using a sharp knife, cut 4 vents in the center of the top crust. Melt the remaining 2 tablespoons butter and brush it on the top of the pie.

Bake until golden brown on top, 45 minutes. Let cool for 20 minutes before serving.

1 large leek (white and tender green parts only), well rinsed and sliced (1 cup)

1 tablespoon olive oil

Salt and freshly ground black pepper

½ cup (1 stick) plus 2 tablespoons unsalted butter

4 small parsnips, peeled and finely chopped (1 cup)

4 medium carrots, finely chopped (2 cups)

1 cup sliced shiitake mushrooms

¼ cup sherry (Dixie likes Harveys Bristol Cream)

½ cup all-purpose flour

2 cups Chicken Stock, homemade (page 45) or store-bought

2 cups heavy cream

4 cups shredded meat from 1 Boiled Chicken (page 45)

1 cup fresh or frozen green peas (thawed if frozen)

1 tablespoon chopped fresh rosemary

1 teaspoon chopped fresh thyme

1 teaspoon chopped fresh tarragon

1 teaspoon white pepper

Dough for 2 (9-inch) pie crusts (see page 202)

CHICKEN, ASPARAGUS, and MUSHROOM CASSEROLE

This casserole is sophisticated enough for a holiday but simple enough that even dedicated nongourmands will enjoy it. Dixie made it last summer for the Rotary Club and we still have Rotarians coming in to scan the casserole selection for this particular dish.

Preheat the oven to 350°F. Spray a 9 × 13-inch baking dish with nonstick cooking spray.

In a large skillet set over medium heat, melt the butter until it just starts to bubble, and then add the mushrooms, asparagus, and garlic. Cook, stirring, until the vegetables are soft, 10 minutes. Whisk in the flour and cook until it becomes golden brown, 3 minutes. Slowly whisk in the Madeira until smooth. Whisk in the stock and cook until smooth and thickened, about 15 minutes. Remove the pan from the heat and stir in the chicken, rice, thyme, tarragon, salt, and white pepper. Scoop the mixture into the prepared baking dish.

Cover with foil and bake for 30 minutes. Uncover and cook until browned on top, 15 more minutes. Let rest for 10 minutes before serving.

½ cup (1 stick) unsalted butter

1 cup sliced shiitake mushrooms

½ bunch asparagus, chopped (1 cup)

1 garlic clove, minced

2 tablespoons all-purpose flour

½ cup Madeira

1 cup Chicken Stock, homemade (page 45) or store-bought

2 cups shredded meat from 1 Boiled Chicken (page 45)

1 cup cooked white rice

1 teaspoon chopped fresh thyme

1 teaspoon chopped fresh tarragon

1 teaspoon kosher salt

½ teaspoon white pepper

Note

This casserole will keep in the freezer for up to 3 months. For best results, freeze it before baking; thaw overnight in the refrigerator, and then bake according to the recipe.

OYSTER CASSEROLE

2 quarts Gulf oysters

½ cup (1 stick) unsalted butter, cut in small pieces

¼ cup dry vermouth

¼ cup chopped green onions (green parts only)

1 (4-ounce) jar diced pimientos, drained

¾ cup heavy cream

2 dashes Tabasco sauce

⅛ teaspoon ground nutmeg

⅛ teaspoon kosher salt

⅛ teaspoon freshly ground black pepper

1 cup crushed Ritz crackers (must use Ritz)

During oyster season, a group of my peers gathers at the Crawdad Hole on Main Street every Friday night. They call in their order for fresh oysters early in the week, pick up cheap champagne (the Crawdad Hole is a brown-bag establishment), and gather to eat oysters with wedges of lemon and lots of laughter. I am not an oyster fan. Dixie and my mother both love them. If you do, make this casserole and pair it with the Asparagus and Strawberry Salad (page 103) for a wonderful and decadent springtime supper.

Preheat the oven to 425°F.

Separate the oysters from the liquid using a strainer (to catch any bits of shell); reserve the liquid.

Spray a 9 × 13-inch casserole dish with nonstick cooking spray. Layer the ingredients in the dish as follows: oysters, ¼ cup of the butter, vermouth, green onions, pimientos, cream, oyster liquid, Tabasco, nutmeg, salt, pepper, crackers, and remaining ¼ cup butter.

Bake until golden brown on top, 30 minutes. This dish will keep for 3 days in the refrigerator. It does not freeze well.

SOUTHWESTERN BEEF CASSEROLE

SERVES 6

This casserole reminds you of how powerfully good classics like meat, cheese, iceberg, and sour cream can be together. Feel free to dial up the hot sauce if you have spice lovers in your midst. Dixie recommends serving this casserole by cutting it into squares, placing them on top of the iceberg lettuce, and dolloping sour cream on the very top.

Preheat the oven to 375°F. Spray a 9 × 13-inch casserole dish with nonstick cooking spray.

In a skillet set over medium-high heat, heat the oil. Add the onion and cook, stirring, until soft, 10 minutes. Add the chuck, garlic, cumin, chili powder, coriander, salt, pepper, cinnamon, and Tabasco. Cook, breaking up the meat with the back of a spoon, until browned through, 10 minutes. Transfer to a paper-towel-lined plate and drain. Transfer the meat mixture to a medium bowl and stir in the corn and tomatoes.

In a saucepan set over medium-high heat, heat the beans with a little water or chicken stock to thin it out and make it spreadable, 5 minutes.

Spread half of the beans in the bottom of the prepared casserole dish. Make a layer with 6 corn tortillas. Top with the remaining refried beans and the Monterey Jack cheese. Make another layer of tortillas, top with the beef mixture, and then the Cheddar cheese.

Cover the dish with foil and bake until the top is golden brown and bubbling, 45 minutes. Let cool for 15 minutes before serving with the lettuce and sour cream.

Note

This casserole will keep in the freezer for up to 3 months. For best results, freeze it before baking; thaw overnight in the refrigerator, and then bake according to the recipe.

1 tablespoon vegetable oil

½ small yellow onion, chopped (¼ cup)

1 pound ground chuck

1 garlic clove, minced

1 tablespoon ground cumin

1 teaspoon chili powder

1 teaspoon ground coriander

1 teaspoon kosher salt

½ teaspoon freshly ground black pepper

⅛ teaspoon ground cinnamon

Dash of Tabasco sauce

1 (14.5-ounce) can cream-style white corn

1 (10-ounce) can mild Ro-tel tomatoes

1 (14.5-ounce) can refried beans

12 white corn tortillas

¼ pound Monterey Jack cheese, shredded (1 cup)

¼ pound sharp Cheddar cheese, shredded (1 cup)

2 cups chopped iceberg lettuce

6 tablespoons sour cream

DIXIE'S LASAGNA

SERVES 6 TO 8

Satisfying and perfect for almost every occasion, it's like an Italian *nonna* made this in her stone kitchen with tomatoes straight from her garden overlooking the Mediterranean. This lasagna is that good.

1 pound dry lasagna noodles

4 tablespoons extra-virgin olive oil, plus more for the noodles

½ cup coarsely chopped yellow onion

¼ cup coarsely chopped green bell pepper

1 garlic clove, minced

1 pound ground chuck

½ pound ground sweet Italian sausage

½ pound ground hot Italian sausage

1 quart whole-milk ricotta cheese

1 egg

1 teaspoon dry vermouth

1 cup chopped fresh spinach

1 tablespoon chopped fresh basil

1 teaspoon freshly ground black pepper

½ teaspoon kosher salt

⅛ teaspoon ground nutmeg

Dash of crushed red pepper flakes

4 cups Marinara Sauce (recipe follows)

½ cup grated Pecorino cheese

1 cup shredded mozzarella

Preheat the oven to 350°F. Spray a 9 × 13-inch casserole dish with nonstick cooking spray.

Cook the noodles according to the package instructions. Drain the noodles and spread them out evenly on a baking sheet, coating them with a little oil so they won't stick. Set aside.

Set a large skillet over medium heat. When hot, add 2 tablespoons of the oil, and then add the onion, bell pepper, and garlic and cook until soft, about 10 minutes. Add the chuck, both sausages, and the remaining 2 tablespoons of oil and cook, breaking up lumps with the back of a spoon, until browned through, about 15 minutes. Transfer to a paper-towel-lined plate to drain.

In a medium bowl, combine the ricotta, egg, vermouth, spinach, basil, pepper, salt, nutmeg, and pepper flakes. Set aside.

Cover the bottom of the prepared casserole dish with just a little marinara sauce and ¼ cup of the Pecorino cheese. Make a layer of lasagna noodles using 3 to 4 noodles lengthwise, and then spread the ricotta mixture evenly over the noodles. Spread 1 cup marinara sauce over the ricotta. Add another layer of noodles, spread the meat mixture evenly over the noodles, cover with 1 cup marinara sauce, and then the mozzarella. Make a final layer of noodles, spread the remaining sauce over the noodles, and top with the remaining ¼ cup Pecorino cheese.

Bake, rotating the dish halfway through, until bubbly, 1 hour. Let sit for 10 to 15 minutes before cutting.

MARINARA SAUCE

MAKES 6 CUPS

In a 4-quart stockpot set over medium heat, heat the oil. Add the onions and cook, stirring, until soft, 10 minutes. Add the garlic and cook for 30 seconds. Add the tomatoes, wine, vinegar, Worcestershire sauce, bay leaves, cinnamon stick, parsley, basil, oregano, thyme, ground fennel, sugar, salt, and pepper. Bring to a low simmer, cover, and cook for 45 minutes, stirring occasionally.

Remove the bay leaves and cinnamon stick before using. The sauce will keep in an airtight container in the refrigerator for 5 days.

¼ cup extra-virgin olive oil

2 tablespoons finely chopped yellow onion

2 garlic cloves, minced

2 (28-ounce) cans diced San Marzano tomatoes, drained

½ cup dry red wine (Dixie recommends a good Chianti)

¼ cup balsamic vinegar

2 tablespoons Worcestershire sauce

2 bay leaves

1 cinnamon stick

2 tablespoons chopped fresh parsley

1 tablespoon chopped fresh basil

1 tablespoon chopped fresh oregano

1 tablespoon chopped fresh thyme

1 teaspoon ground fennel

1 teaspoon sugar

1 teaspoon kosher salt

½ teaspoon freshly ground black pepper

Note
This casserole will keep in the freezer for up to 3 months. For best results, freeze it before baking; thaw overnight in the refrigerator, and then bake according to the recipe.

Mains

ROASTED PORK TENDERLOIN *with*
APRICOT-APPLE CIDER GLAZE

BEEF STROGANOFF

GRILLADES

HOME-BRINED CORNED BEEF BRISKET

SHEPHERD'S PIE

DIXIE'S TURKEY MEAT LOAF
with MUSHROOM GRAVY

HONEY PECAN CATFISH

BLACKENED CATFISH
with TABASCO BEURRE BLANC

CHANDELEUR ISLANDS SPECKLED TROUT

CRAB CAKES *with* DILL TARTAR SAUCE

BAKED GULF SHRIMP IN LEMON SHALLOT
GARLIC BUTTER

SHRIMP *and* GRITS

COULTER'S RED BEANS *and* RICE

ROASTED PORK TENDERLOIN *with* Apricot-Apple Cider Glaze

SERVES 6 TO 8

Right now I have four pigs fattening in the yard. My children are unrepentant carnivores, but on the plus side, they are entirely clear about where food comes from. One day, as we talked about what to have for dinner, Annaliese observed that we didn't have any chicken in the fridge, so she guessed we'd have to go out back and kill one.

Unlike industrially raised pork, which is one of the more stomach-turning agricultural experiments in our country, my pigs eat everything from hog grain from the feed store to my kids' uneaten cereal to the corn bread we fail to sell at lunch. They eat speckled black bananas, béchamel sauce, leftover pancakes from customers' plates, yellowing cabbage, orange peels—the works.

If you have access to some good pork from pigs who led fat and happy lives, this is a wonderful holiday meal that combines the sweetness of apricots with the interest of apple cider and the savory of roasted pork. I recommend serving alongside the Roasted Green Beans with Sweet Peppers (page 184) and the Roasted Fennel Mashed Potatoes (page 181).

2 pork tenderloins (each 2 pounds)

Extra-virgin olive oil

Kosher salt and freshly ground black pepper

2 tablespoons dried basil

1 tablespoon chopped fresh thyme

2 teaspoons sugar

1 cup apricot preserves

½ cup apple cider

1 tablespoon brandy

1 tablespoon apple cider vinegar (Dixie prefers the Bragg brand)

Preheat the oven to 400°F.

Rub the pork tenderloins with the oil, and season with salt and pepper. Put them on a rack set over a baking sheet and sprinkle with the basil, thyme, and sugar.

Roast until the pork is medium (160°F on a meat thermometer), 20 minutes. Remove the pan from the oven and let the pork rest for 10 minutes before slicing.

Meanwhile, in a saucepan set over medium heat, combine the preserves, cider, brandy, and vinegar. Cook, whisking constantly, until reduced by half, 10 minutes.

To serve, divide the pork among serving plates and drizzle the sauce over the top.

BEEF STROGANOFF

¼ cup extra-virgin olive oil

1¾ pounds sirloin roast, cut into 2-inch cubes

4 tablespoons (½ stick) unsalted butter

1 small yellow onion, chopped (½ cup)

1 medium carrot, chopped (½ cup)

1 pound white mushrooms, sliced

1 garlic clove, minced

1 tablespoon all-purpose flour

4 cups beef stock

¼ cup brandy

¼ cup dry red wine

½ cup heavy cream

1 cup sour cream

1 tablespoon tomato paste

1 tablespoon Worcestershire sauce

1 teaspoon Djjon mustard

3 tablespoons chopped fresh parsley

1 tablespoon chopped fresh thyme

1 tablespoon chopped fresh rosemary

½ teaspoon freshly ground black pepper

Kosher salt

1 (12-ounce) package wide egg noodles

Who wouldn't be happy to walk through the door on a chilly evening to find beef stroganoff on the table? Savory, evocative of a simpler time, this dinner is sure to be a big hit.

In a Dutch oven set over medium heat, heat the oil until hot, about 3 minutes. Add the sirloin and cook until browned on all sides, 10 to 15 minutes. Using a slotted spoon, transfer it to a plate and set aside.

To the pan, add 2 tablespoons of the butter, the onions, carrots, mushrooms, and garlic. Cook, stirring, until soft, 10 minutes. Sprinkle the flour over the vegetables and cook, stirring constantly, until no lumps remain, 5 more minutes. Add the stock, brandy, and red wine, bring to a low simmer, and return the beef to the pot. Add the cream, ½ cup of the sour cream, the tomato paste, Worcestershire sauce, mustard, 2 tablespoons of the parsley, the thyme, rosemary, and pepper. Season to taste with salt. Cover and simmer on low heat for 2 hours, stirring occasionally.

Cook the egg noodles according to the package instructions. Toss with the remaining 2 tablespoons butter and 1 tablespoon parsley.

Serve the stroganoff on top of the noodles, with a dollop of sour cream.

GRILLADES

SERVES 6

In Mississippi, hints of our Creole cousins show up on menus all over town. Grillades is a traditional New Orleans dish of beef cooked with vegetables, typically served with grits—use Dixie's Three-Cheese Grits recipe—at breakfast or brunch. Sprinkle each serving with some chopped green onions if you want to dress it up a touch.

In a large skillet or Dutch oven set over medium heat, heat the butter and oil until it starts to bubble, 5 minutes. Whisk in the flour to make a roux and cook over medium heat, whisking constantly, until dark brown, 10 to 15 minutes. Add the onion, bell pepper, celery, and garlic and cook, stirring constantly, until soft, 10 minutes. Whisk in the red wine, followed by the stock, whisking until there are no lumps and it has thickened, about 15 minutes. Add the steak, tomatoes, Worcestershire sauce, balsamic vinegar, Tabasco, parsley, rosemary, thyme, onion powder, garlic powder, Creole seasoning, salt, and pepper. Bring to a simmer, reduce the heat to low, cover, and cook for 2 hours, stirring occasionally.

Serve over the cheese grits and garnish with the scallions.

¼ cup (½ stick) unsalted butter

¼ cup extra-virgin olive oil

¼ cup all-purpose flour

1 large yellow onion, chopped (1 cup)

1 large red bell pepper, cored, seeded, and chopped (1 cup)

2 tablespoons chopped celery hearts

2 garlic cloves, minced

1 cup dry red wine

2 cups beef stock

2 pounds round steak, cut into 2-inch pieces

1 (14.5-ounce) can petite diced tomatoes, drained

2 tablespoons Worcestershire sauce

1 tablespoon balsamic vinegar

1 tablespoon Tabasco sauce

2 tablespoons chopped fresh parsley

2 tablespoons chopped fresh rosemary

2 tablespoons chopped fresh thyme

2 tablespoons onion powder

1 tablespoon garlic powder

1 tablespoon Creole seasoning

1 teaspoon kosher salt

½ teaspoon freshly ground black pepper

Three-Cheese Grits (page 26)

Home-brined CORNED BEEF BRISKET

SERVES 6 TO 8

1 cup white vinegar

2 cups kosher salt

1 cup granulated sugar

1 cup packed light brown sugar

¼ cup premixed pickling spices, such as McCormick

4 bay leaves

2 cinnamon sticks

2 teaspoons yellow mustard seeds

2 teaspoons whole cloves

2 teaspoons whole black peppercorns

1 teaspoon ground allspice

1 teaspoon ground ginger

½ teaspoon crushed red pepper flakes

1 beef brisket (5 to 7 pounds)

1 yellow onion, quartered

2 large carrots, cut in half

2 celery stalks, cut in half

6 garlic cloves

In the kitchen of the B.T.C. lurks the world's largest Tupperware container. It looks like a sweater box, and Dixie uses it for ten or so days out of the year. Her only use for it is to fill it with pounds and pounds of beef brisket, water, vinegar, and specially ordered pickling spices. It sits on a shelf in the refrigerator and fills the cold air with the smell of pickles. And then, on St. Patty's day, she serves it with cabbage, carrots, and new potatoes in an advertised lunch special that packs our cafe so full it's nearly busting its seams. (It is Kagan's favorite lunch of the year; he is invariably our first customer.)

The brisket is worth the buildup: so tender, it flakes apart with a fork. Brining your own corned beef is very simple and is an enormous crowd-pleaser that confers serious bragging rights. Just don't skip the ten days of brining that Dixie recommends. Slice it thinly and serve it alongside Creamed Cabbage with Sherry (page 180) or Root Vegetable Mash (page 193).

In an 8-quart stockpot, combine 4 quarts of water with the vinegar, salt, granulated and brown sugars, pickling spices, bay leaves, cinnamon sticks, mustard seeds, cloves, peppercorns, allspice, ginger, and red pepper flakes. Bring to a boil over high heat, stirring occasionally with a whisk. Once the salt and sugar have dissolved, remove the pot from the heat and let cool completely, about 4 hours.

Put the brisket in a large plastic container with a lid, fat side up. Cover the meat completely with the cooled brining liquid (the meat must be completely covered). Weight it down with several bowls or plates, cover tightly with the lid, and refrigerate for 10 days.

After 10 days, remove the beef from the brine and rinse it thoroughly. Put the brisket in an 8- to 10-quart stockpot, cover with water, and add the onion, carrots, celery, and garlic. Bring to a boil. Reduce the heat to a low simmer, cover, and cook for 4 hours.

Remove the brisket from the water and let it sit for 15 minutes. Slice thinly and serve.

SHEPHERD'S PIE

SERVES 6

Shepherd's pie is one of those international comfort foods, like some form of pasta with some form of cheese. Seriously. The French have a version, the South American countries have *pastel de papa*, and even Puerto Ricans make a meat-based dish topped with potatoes. I adore this dish. Shepherd's pie taps into my love of Wellingtons, rainy days, and large gray woolen cardigans. (Why, yes, sometimes I like to pretend, in my head, that I am British. You?)

This particular version calls for two cups of the Roasted Fennel Mashed Potatoes, so it's either a great way to use up the rest of your mashed potatoes or a good excuse to make them to begin with.

1 tablespoon extra-virgin oil

2 medium carrots, chopped (1 cup)

1 small turnip, peeled and chopped (1 cup)

2 small parsnips, peeled and chopped (½ cup)

1 pound ground lamb

1 garlic clove, minced

¼ cup dark beer, such as Guinness

1 cup beef stock

1 cup frozen pearl onions, thawed

1 cup frozen green peas, thawed

2 tablespoons tomato paste

1 teaspoon Worcestershire sauce

1 tablespoon chopped fresh thyme

1 tablespoon chopped fresh rosemary

1 tablespoon chopped fresh parsley

1 teaspoon ground fennel

1 teaspoon kosher salt

1 teaspoon freshly ground black pepper

2 cups Roasted Fennel Mashed Potatoes (page 181)

Preheat the oven to 375°F. Spray a 9 × 13-inch baking dish with nonstick cooking spray.

In a large skillet or Dutch oven set over medium heat, heat the oil. Add the carrots, turnip, and parsnips and cook, stirring, until soft, 10 minutes. Using a slotted spoon, transfer the vegetables to a plate and set aside.

In the same skillet, cook the lamb and garlic until browned through, 10 minutes. Add the beer and cook until reduced by half, 10 minutes. Add the stock and bring to a low simmer. Add the cooked vegetables, onions, peas, tomato paste, Worcestershire sauce, thyme, rosemary, parsley, fennel, salt, and pepper. Cook until it returns to a low simmer, 10 minutes. Pour into the prepared baking dish.

Spoon the mashed potatoes into a pastry bag fitted with a star tip and cover the lamb mixture with rosettes (you can also simply spoon them on the lamb and smooth the top with a spatula).

Bake until the potatoes are golden brown, 45 minutes.

DIXIE'S TURKEY MEAT LOAF *with* MUSHROOM GRAVY

SERVES 4

Being a professional chef, Dixie makes things to please people who are interested in things that she personally doesn't have much stake in. Like health. Dixie is all about good food, but she drinks a can of Tab every morning for breakfast and spends her tip money on high-end beer and cigarettes. Cholesterol isn't one of her concerns.

But dry meat loaf, on the other hand, is. She created this meat loaf to please the customers who eschew red meat, and in doing so, she made sure it was moist and savory enough to please her inner gourmand.

Preheat the oven to 375°F.

For the meat loaf, in a sauté pan set over medium heat, heat the oil. Add the onion, bell pepper, and mushrooms and cook, stirring, until the onion is caramelized, 13 minutes. Transfer the vegetables to a large bowl. Add the turkey, bread crumbs, garlic, eggs, ketchup, Worcestershire sauce, wine, granulated garlic, granulated onion, and pepper. Season with salt. Using your hands, mix thoroughly.

Scoop the mixture into an 8 × 8-inch baking dish and spread it out evenly. Bake until the internal temperature reaches 170°F, 45 to 60 minutes. Let cool for 10 minutes before serving.

For the gravy, meanwhile, in a sauté pan set over medium heat, heat the oil. Add the mushrooms and cook, stirring, until soft, 10 minutes. Add the butter, and when it has melted, gradually whisk in the flour. Cook, whisking constantly, for 1 minute. Whisk in the stock until smooth and cook until the desired thickness, about 15 minutes. Season with salt and pepper.

To serve, slice into squares and top with the gravy.

MEAT LOAF

2 tablespoons extra-virgin olive oil

1 medium onion, finely chopped

1 small green bell pepper, cored, seeded, and finely chopped

1 cup chopped button mushrooms

2 pounds ground turkey

1 cup panko bread crumbs

1 garlic clove, crushed

2 eggs, beaten

3 tablespoons ketchup

3 tablespoons Worcestershire sauce

1 tablespoon dry red wine

1 tablespoon granulated garlic

1 tablespoon granulated onion

⅛ teaspoon freshly ground black pepper

Salt

MUSHROOM GRAVY

1 tablespoon extra-virgin olive oil

1 cup sliced button mushrooms

2 tablespoons unsalted butter

2 tablespoons all-purpose flour

1½ cups beef stock

Salt

⅛ teaspoon freshly ground black pepper

HONEY PECAN CATFISH

SERVES 4

1 cup extra-virgin olive oil

½ cup local honey

2 tablespoons hazelnut liqueur, such as Frangelico

2 tablespoons apple cider vinegar (Dixie prefers the Bragg brand)

½ cup chopped pecans

1 clove garlic, chopped

1 teaspoon crushed red pepper flakes

1 teaspoon ground cinnamon

1 teaspoon ground allspice

1 teaspoon ground anise

½ teaspoon ground cloves

½ teaspoon ground mace

Salt and freshly ground black pepper

4 catfish fillets, such as Pride of the Pond (each 7 to 9 ounces)

Honey, pecans, catfish. Could this dish be more Mississippi if it tried? Dixie tells me that it was one of the most popular dishes she created at the fancy restaurant in her past. The catfish marinates in the sweet, spiced mixture of honey and pecan and then caramelizes during baking.

While we're on the subject of catfish, let's be clear: not all catfish is created equal. Make sure you're buying fish raised in America, not overseas. Spring for a higher-end brand (Dixie swears by Pride of the Pond) because catfish can taste muddy if poorly raised.

Serve this with Roasted Green Beans with Sweet Peppers (page 184).

In a large bowl, whisk together the oil, honey, liqueur, vinegar, pecans, garlic, pepper flakes, cinnamon, allspice, anise, cloves, and mace, and season to taste with salt and black pepper. Add the catfish and coat well. Cover the bowl with plastic wrap and refrigerate overnight.

Preheat the oven to 425°F. Spray a round or square baking sheet with nonstick cooking spray.

Take the catfish out of the refrigerator and lay the fillets on the prepared baking sheet. Bake until the catfish flakes in the center, 25 to 35 minutes.

Serve immediately.

BLACKENED CATFISH *with* *Tabasco Beurre Blanc*

SERVES 4

Blackened fish is hip because it is tasty and it is healthy. Unfortunately, Dixie blows the health benefits out of the water with the beurre blanc, which is a French concoction of butter and wine that manages to be light and airy but still heavy enough to cling to the fish. The texture is fantastic—spicy and silkily smooth—and will impress the pants off of whomever you're eating dinner with.

FISH

1 small red onion, thinly sliced

1 small green bell pepper, cored, seeded, and julienned

1 bottle dark beer, such as Guinness

1 cup extra-virgin olive oil

1 cup yellow mustard

1 tablespoon fresh lime juice

¼ cup Blackening Seasoning (page 56)

4 catfish fillets, such as Pride of the Pond (each 7 to 9 ounces)

BEURRE BLANC

½ cup Tabasco sauce

½ cup dry white wine

2 tablespoons fresh lime juice

1 shallot, finely chopped

1 garlic clove, minced

2 cups (4 sticks) unsalted butter, cut into cubes and at room temperature

Salt and freshly ground black pepper

For the catfish, in a large bowl, combine the onion, bell pepper, beer, oil, mustard, lime juice, and Blackening Seasoning. Add the catfish, cover the bowl with plastic wrap, and refrigerate overnight.

Preheat the oven to 425°F. Spray a baking sheet with nonstick cooking spray.

Take the catfish out of the refrigerator and put it on the prepared baking sheet. (Do not drain it from the marinade.) Bake until the fish flakes in the center, 25 to 35 minutes.

Meanwhile, make the *beurre blanc.* In a saucepan set over high heat, combine the Tabasco, wine, lime juice, shallot, and garlic. Cook until the liquid has reduced by half, 10 minutes. Remove the pan from the heat and immediately start whisking in the butter, a few pieces at a time, until the mixture is creamy. Season with salt and pepper to taste.

To serve, put a fillet on each of 4 serving plates. Top with the beurre blanc and serve immediately.

Chandeleur Islands
SPECKLED TROUT

SERVES 4

Cliff is a sixty-something gentleman with a handlebar mustache and killer abs and is married to a lovely lady named Ramona. He's also one of Kagan's best friends and continually entices Kagan on adventures: They have kayaked the Mississippi, taken Annaliese to a gun show, and once, memorably, gone on a fishing excursion in the Gulf of Mexico where they narrowly escaped a shark attack (small sharks) on a chain of small islands called the Chandeleurs.

Kagan irritates and intimidates folks near and far with his prowess at renovations, presentations, pie baking, pickle making, and all other sorts of skills. Yet, he is the worst sportsman in the world. He once took the kids fishing, and in three hours the only time he had so much as a nibble was when they jabbed the poles into the bank to take a ten-minute nature walk and returned to find one missing. Accomplished hunters take him into the woods, promising that it's a sure thing, and with Kagan there, they see absolutely nothing.

On their three-day chartered-boat fishing expedition, Kagan's bad luck held, and despite earnestly fishing from sunup to sundown, he caught nothing he could keep. Cliff sweetly shared his catch and sent Kagan home with sealed plastic bags of filleted fish and instructions on how to cook it (spoiler: remarkably quick, remarkably easy, remarkably good). I ate this fish, marveling at its tender flavor while laughing at Kagan's sporting tales. Keep it simple and serve with Caraway Dill Biscuits (page 17) and Asparagus and Strawberry Salad (page 103).

Olive oil

4 speckled trout fillets (each 6 to 8 ounces)

4 teaspoons fresh lemon juice

1 small onion, finely chopped

2 tablespoons chopped fresh parsley

1 teaspoon sweet paprika

Salt and freshly ground black pepper

Preheat the oven to 400°F.

Put each trout fillet on a lightly oiled square of aluminum foil that's twice the size of the fish. Divide the lemon juice, onion, parsley, and paprika among the fillets, and season each to taste with salt and pepper. Fold up the foil squares, sealing the edges to create packets. Put the packets on a baking sheet.

Bake until the fish is cooked and flakes apart at the touch of a fork, 15 to 18 minutes.

CRAB CAKES
with Dill Tartar Sauce

SERVES 4

Dixie makes these, usually letting Annaliese empty the cans of crabmeat. Dixie arranges two on a tray, wraps them in Saran Wrap, and slaps on a label that reads "Dixie's Idiot-Proof Crab Cakes," with two sentences of cooking instructions. We stack them up in the cooler, and they sell like hotcakes.

These crab cakes are so good that just one on its own, maybe with a crisp green salad, will do the trick for a nice dinner. But if you want your mind blown, try one on top of Dixie's Three-Cheese Grits (page 26). Be careful whom you serve it to, because they may never leave.

Preheat the oven to 500°F.

In a large bowl, combine the lump crabmeat and claw meat, celery, all the bell peppers, onions, mayonnaise, mustard, Worcestershire sauce, lemon juice, vermouth, Tabasco, tarragon, and Old Bay, trying to keep as much of the jumbo lump crabmeat intact as possible.

Put the bread crumbs in a bowl. Roll the crab mixture into 4 evenly sized balls, and then roll in the bread crumbs. Shape the balls into thick patties (do not flatten out).

In a large oven-safe skillet, melt the butter. Put 3 to 4 patties in the pan and cook until browned on one side, about 7 minutes. Turn them over and brown the second side, 7 minutes. Transfer the pan to the oven and bake for 10 minutes, until golden brown and crispy.

Divide among 4 plates, top with the tartar sauce, and serve immediately.

1 pound canned jumbo lump crabmeat

1 pound canned crab claw meat

3 celery hearts, finely chopped (½ cup)

¼ cup finely chopped yellow bell pepper

¼ cup finely chopped red bell pepper

¼ cup finely chopped green bell pepper

1 bunch green onions, sliced

½ cup Hellmann's mayonnaise

1 tablespoon Dijon mustard

1 tablespoon Worcestershire sauce

1 teaspoon fresh lemon juice

1 teaspoon dry vermouth

Dash of Tabasco sauce

2 tablespoons dried tarragon

2 tablespoons Old Bay seasoning

1 cup panko bread crumbs

2 tablespoons unsalted butter

Dill Tartar Sauce (recipe follows)

DILL TARTAR SAUCE

2 cups Hellmann's mayonnaise

2 tablespoons fresh lime juice

1 teaspoon Worcestershire sauce

1½ teaspoons Dijon mustard

Dash of Tabasco sauce

¼ cup minced sweet onions

1 teaspoon minced green bell
    pepper

¼ cup dill pickle relish

2 tablespoons sweet pickle relish

1 tablespoon chopped fresh dill

1 teaspoon granulated garlic

⅛ teaspoon kosher salt

⅛ teaspoon white pepper

MAKES 2¼ CUPS

Accompanies the crab cakes, but if you're felling ambitious for a quick kid-friendly supper, I can tell you from personal experience it dresses up fish sticks quite nicely, too.

In a medium bowl, whisk together the mayonnaise, lime juice, Worcestershire sauce, mustard, and Tabasco. Fold in the onion, bell pepper, and both relishes. Add the dill, granulated garlic, salt, and white pepper, and lightly whisk until well blended. The dill sauce will keep in an airtight container for up to 4 days.

Baked GULF SHRIMP in Lemon Shallot Garlic Butter

SERVES 4

We spend most of our vacation time visiting family in Virginia and Vermont, but at the beginning of shrimp season along the Gulf Coast, Kagan and I point our battered station wagon south and drive with our kids to Biloxi for a long weekend. The kids play on the beach, we eat shrimp caught that morning, and there's always a watermelon on ice in a cooler. We love fresh shrimp, and this is a fantastic way to eat it. It's like shrimp scampi without the distraction of pasta.

Preheat the oven to 425°F.

In a shallow baking dish, lay the shrimp in a single layer, head to tail.

In a medium bowl, combine the butter, white wine, lemon juice, shallots, garlic, parsley, salt, white pepper, and pepper flakes. Pour the mixture over the shrimp, and sprinkle the bread crumbs over the top.

Bake until the shrimp are pink and the bread crumbs are golden brown, 15 to 20 minutes.

Serve immediately.

1 pound tail-on, peeled, and deveined Gulf shrimp

2 cups (4 sticks) unsalted butter, melted

¼ cup dry white wine

2 tablespoons fresh lemon juice

¼ cup minced shallots

4 garlic cloves, minced

2 tablespoons chopped fresh parsley

1 teaspoon salt

⅛ teaspoon white pepper

Dash of crushed red pepper flakes

1 cup panko bread crumbs

SHRIMP *and Grits*

2 tablespoons unsalted butter

2 tablespoons extra-virgin olive oil

2 tablespoons chopped yellow
onion

2 tablespoons chopped red bell
pepper

2 tablespoons chopped celery
hearts

2 tablespoons chopped andouille
sausage

2 tablespoons chopped tasso ham

1 garlic clove, minced

¼ cup dry white wine

½ cup Chicken Stock, homemade
(page 45) or store-bought

1 bay leaf

1 teaspoon chopped fresh parsley

½ teaspoon chopped fresh thyme

½ teaspoon cayenne pepper

1 teaspoon salt

1 pound large Gulf shrimp, peeled
and deveined

Dixie's Three-Cheese Grits
(page 26)

SERVES 4

This meal is so ridiculously scrumptious. Make it. Enjoy it. Scrape off every spoonful, and then, even if someone's watching, go ahead and lick the plate. If they're eating with you, they'll understand. It's just that good.

In a large skillet set over medium heat, heat the butter and oil. Add the onion, bell pepper, and celery and cook, stirring, until soft, 10 minutes. Add the sausage and tasso and cook, stirring, for 5 more minutes. Add the garlic and wine and cook until the wine is reduced by half, 5 minutes. Add the stock, bay leaf, parsley, thyme, cayenne, and salt. Cook on low heat until simmering, 10 minutes. Add the shrimp and cook until they turn pink and start to curl, 5 to 7 minutes. Remove the bay leaf.

Serve immediately on top of cheese grits.

Coulter's RED BEANS and RICE

SERVES 6 TO 8

2 pounds dry red beans

3 or 4 green bell peppers

3 tablespoons bacon grease

1 ham hock or ½ pound tasso ham

1½ large Vidalia onions, chopped

3 celery hearts, chopped (½ cup)

1 pound andouille sausage

1 garlic clove

Leaves from the celery bunch, chopped

1 bay leaf

1 teaspoon dried thyme

1 teaspoon dried parsley

1 teaspoon Slap Ya Mama Cajun seasoning

1 teaspoon chili powder

1 teaspoon cayenne pepper

6 cups Chicken Stock, homemade (page 45) or store-bought, or water

Salt and freshly ground black pepper

Perfect White Rice (page 198)

Note

You can easily make this recipe vegetarian by leaving out all the meat, using water instead of stock, and using oil instead of bacon grease. It'll still taste really good.

Coulter Fussell is my closest counterpart in Water Valley: two kids, old house, business just two doors down from mine. Unlike me, she has serious hipster credentials. Her entire family is ridiculously accomplished, and she counts iconic musicians and artists as family friends. She upped and married Amos Harvey a while back, an engaging and intriguing fellow who spends his time managing the tours of bands like Hot Chip and hangs out with famous people in foreign places on a regular basis.

I asked her for this recipe because I heard her describe the process to Penelope Green, the writer of the *New York Times* article that changed all our lives, and I've never forgotten how good it sounded. She said that red beans and rice isn't an exact science. The recipe may look long and involved, but in practice it's just grabbing things, chopping them, and throwing them into a big pot. The important part is that you drink red wine with your company and talk about people while stirring the pot. That makes it taste better. She likes to make red beans on Sunday, store them in the refrigerator, and eat them on Monday. They also freeze very well. This is a big recipe, and Coulter usually freezes about a third of it.

Put the beans in a large pot and cover with water. Soak overnight.

Roast the bell peppers over the flame of a gas burner, turning them until they are blackened on all sides. Put them in a paper bag, close the top, and let them steam for about 10 minutes. Peel off and discard the blackened skin. Seed and chop the peppers, catching and reserving as much of the juice as you can. Set aside.

Drain the beans and set aside. Put the bacon grease in the pot and set the pot over medium heat. If you're using tasso, add it to the pan and cook for 2 minutes; transfer to a plate. Add the roasted peppers, onions, and celery. Cook, stirring, until the onions are soft and translucent, about 10 minutes. Crumble half of the sausage and add it to the pot with the tasso and ham hock (if using), garlic, celery leaves, bay leaf, thyme, parsley, Cajun seasoning, chili powder, cayenne, and beans. Cook, stirring, for 2 to 3 minutes. Add the juices from the roasted bell peppers and enough stock to cover the beans. Bring to a boil. Reduce the heat to low, cover the pot halfway, and cook for 2 hours, occasionally stirring vigorously. Mash some beans on the side of the pot with the back of the spoon to give it a good texture. After about 1 hour 30 minutes, if you used the ham hock, remove it, let it cool, pull the meat from it, and put the meat back in. Discard the hock. Season to taste with salt and pepper.

Right before serving, slice the remaining sausage and fry the slices in a skillet set over medium heat until browned on both sides and a little crunchy, 10 to 12 minutes. Drain on a paper towel.

To serve, put a little of the rice in a bowl and spoon a lot of red beans on top. Put fried sausage on top of that.

Friend and Neighbor:
ALSO, THE REASON I HAVE ART IN MY LIFE

Coulter spends her days at her business, Yalo Studio and Gallery, which has managed to make folks like me, who were previously completely uninterested in art, attend gallery openings and buy original works on a regular basis. Yalo is tiny: about ten feet wide and fifty feet deep. Four to six times a year, that small gallery packs Main Street with people from near and far, thronging to see shows such as:

1. The po'boy photos of a "serious" artist (Chris Sullivan) paired with the beautifully framed found hair weaves of Coulter's brother. Who, as it turns out, has found a lot of strange people's hair weaves.
2. For the annual World's Largest Crappie Festival, Coulter had work up by an internationally renowned artist named Derek Hess, which featured crappie fish with bomber squadron paraphernalia painted on and around them.
3. My personal favorite: 102 identical and original paintings by artist Mike Howard. Buy one of the paintings (which were of peaches, by the by) for fifty dollars and you were automatically entered to win a sweepstakes. The ten prizes ranged from New Year's in New Orleans to breakfast at the B.T.C. If you bought a single painting, you had just over a one in ten chance of winning. And regardless, you went home with a painting.

In other words, Coulter is innovative in a big way. She's also an artist in her own right and the painting of the eight-year-old girl in her underwear waving a red flag at a bull that hangs in her living room has been a source of envy for years. Her husband, Amos, won't let her part with it.

Sides

CREAMED CABBAGE *with* SHERRY

ROASTED FENNEL MASHED POTATOES

SUMMER STUFFED ZUCCHINI

ROASTED GREEN BEANS
with SWEET PEPPERS

BAKED GREEN BEANS
with WILD MUSHROOMS

CREAMY LEEKS IN MORNAY SAUCE

YELLOW SQUASH AU GRATIN

BAKED SQUASH *with* VIDALIA ONIONS

CRABMEAT-STUFFED MUSHROOMS

ROOT VEGETABLE MASH

CLIFF'S HOMINY SAN JUAN

FETACHOKE CUPS

CORN BREAD DRESSING

PERFECT WHITE RICE

CREAMED CABBAGE *with Sherry*

SERVES 6

6 strips thick-cut apple-wood
smoked bacon, chopped

1 large yellow onion, thinly sliced
(1 cup)

½ cup sherry (Dixie likes Harveys
Bristol Cream)

2 tablespoons apple cider vinegar
(Dixie prefers the Bragg brand)

6 cups shredded Savoy cabbage

¼ cup Chicken Stock, homemade
(page 45) or store-bought

1 teaspoon sugar

¼ teaspoon kosher salt

⅛ teaspoon freshly ground black
pepper

⅛ teaspoon crushed red pepper
flakes

1 cup heavy cream

I never ate much cabbage before moving to Mississippi. It is cheap, nutritious,
readily available. In fact, I have a large head sitting on my counter right now,
crying out for some attention. This particular recipe pairs wonderfully with
our Home-brined Corned Beef Brisket (page 162).

In a large skillet set over medium-high heat, cook the bacon until
the fat is rendered, 3 to 4 minutes. Add the onion and cook,
stirring, until soft, 5 minutes. Add the sherry and vinegar and cook,
stirring, until the liquid has reduced by half, 5 minutes. Add the
cabbage and stir, coating it well with the onion mixture. Add the
stock, sugar, salt, black pepper and red pepper flakes. Cover the
pan and cook until the cabbage is tender, 15 to 20 minutes. Remove
the lid and add the heavy cream. Cook on low heat until the cream
is reduced by half, 10 minutes. Serve immediately.

Roasted Fennel
MASHED POTATOES

SERVES 4 TO 6

Our neighbor, friend, and acclaimed gardener, Miss Anne, was in the store the other day, telling Dixie about her fennel harvest. I saw Dixie's eyes light up. She loves fennel. She's not alone: Andres and Carolyn, noted photographers who lived in Istanbul for several years and now live (in between their international photography gigs) in the loft apartment over the B.T.C., also adore the underrated vegetable. They buy fennel whenever we have some, cut it into thin slices, and eat it raw. In this mashed potato recipe, fennel lends a clean and sophisticated taste that pairs wonderfully with the Roasted Pork Tenderloin with Apricot–Apple Cider Glaze (page 159).

1 large fennel bulb, thinly sliced (1½ cups)

2 tablespoons extra-virgin olive oil

4 sprigs fresh thyme

Salt

Freshly ground black pepper

3½ pounds Yukon gold potatoes, peeled and chopped

1 cup heavy cream

¼ cup (½ stick) unsalted butter

2 tablespoons sour cream

½ teaspoon white pepper

Preheat the oven to 400°F.

In a bowl, toss together the fennel and oil. Spread the fennel out evenly in a baking dish, lay the thyme sprigs on top, and season with salt and pepper. Roast until the fennel is soft and golden brown, 20 to 30 minutes. Remove the pan from the oven and set aside.

Put the potatoes in an 8-quart stockpot, season with a little salt, and cover with water. Set the pot over high heat. Bring to a boil and cook until the potatoes are soft, 15 minutes.

Meanwhile, heat the cream and butter in a saucepan set over medium-low heat until just warm, 5 to 7 minutes. Leave on the stove until you're ready to use it.

Drain the potatoes and return them to the warm pot. Mash them with a handheld potato masher. Add the cream and butter mixture, sour cream, white pepper, and ½ teaspoon salt.

Chop the roasted fennel and stir it into the potatoes. Serve hot.

SUMMER STUFFED ZUCCHINI

Last summer, Miz Zandra Walker brought me a massive zucchini she'd hollowed out and turned into a centerpiece by stuffing it with zinnias and other summer flowers. It sat on top of our deli cooler for a good four days, delighting customers and causing a great deal more commotion than a zucchini in July tends to do.

Zucchini, for you nongardeners out there, can be frighteningly prolific and grow inches overnight. Luckily, there's a host of ways to cook this vegetable: I've seen it in salads, soups, fritters, bread, and here, stuffed in a different way, but no less summery or delightful.

6 small zucchini

6 green onions, coarsely chopped

1 carrot, cut into chunks

1 celery heart, coarsely chopped

½ red bell pepper, cored, seeded, and coarsely chopped

1 shallot, quartered

1 garlic clove, coarsely chopped

¼ cup (½ stick) unsalted butter

1 cup panko bread crumbs

1 teaspoon dried basil

⅛ teaspoon freshly ground black pepper

1 egg, beaten

½ cup grated Parmesan cheese

Salt

Cut the zucchini in half and scoop out the flesh. Set the zucchini shells aside, and put the flesh in a food processor. Add the onions, carrot, celery, bell pepper, shallot, and garlic and pulse until finely chopped.

In a large sauté pan set over medium heat, melt the butter. Add the chopped vegetable mixture and cook, stirring, until soft, 13 minutes. Add the bread crumbs, basil, and pepper, and reduce the heat to low. Add the egg and cook, stirring, for 1 minute. Remove the pan from the heat. Add ¼ cup of the cheese and stir well. Season with salt to taste.

Fill the zucchini shells with the stuffing and put them in a shallow baking dish. Top with the remaining ¼ cup cheese. Bake for 20 to 25 minutes, until the tops are golden brown and the zucchini are fork-tender.

ROASTED GREEN BEANS *with* SWEET PEPPERS

SERVES 4

1 pound fresh green beans, ends trimmed and strings removed

1 red bell pepper, cored, seeded, and thickly sliced

1 yellow bell pepper, cored, seeded, and thickly sliced

1 small Vidalia onion, thickly sliced

¼ cup extra-virgin olive oil

1½ teaspoons kosher salt

1 teaspoon freshly ground black pepper

1 fresh lime, cut in half

Kagan and I both had to pick bush beans as kids. For those of you nongardeners, eatin' beans are commonly grown as either pole varieties (long vines that wrap around trellises or poles to grow up high) or as bush varieties (easier to manage; murder on the back).

If you have some young ones you're looking to scar for the rest of their lives, plant some beans. Send them picking. And then make this recipe and they just may forgive you: Crunchy, savory, and satisfying, it is the perfect side dish for a summer supper and pairs nicely with the Honey Pecan Catfish (page 166).

Preheat the oven to 425°F.

In a large bowl, combine the green beans, bell peppers, and onions. Add the oil, salt, and pepper and toss well. Spread out in a single layer on a baking sheet.

Roast until golden brown and starting to caramelize, 30 to 40 minutes. Remove the pan from the oven and squeeze the lime over the top. Serve immediately.

BAKED GREEN BEANS *with* WILD MUSHROOMS

SERVES 4 TO 6

This side is good year-round. High-class enough for Christmas dinner, simple enough for Sunday night supper, it is a wonderful way to pair crisp beans with velvety mushrooms. Dixie likes to top hers with very thinly sliced fried onion rings for extra crunch, but the side dish is absolutely fine without them as well.

½ cup (1 stick) unsalted butter

2 teaspoons all-purpose flour

1½ cups Chicken Stock, homemade (page 45) or store bought

Pinch of ground nutmeg

Salt and freshly ground black pepper

2 tablespoons extra-virgin olive oil

1 shallot, finely chopped

1 pound fresh green beans, ends trimmed and strings removed

1 garlic clove, chopped

¼ cup sliced shiitake mushrooms

¼ cup sliced baby portabella mushrooms

¼ cup sliced chanterelle mushrooms

2 tablespoons sherry (Dixie prefers Harveys Bristol Cream)

Preheat the oven to 375°F. Spray a 9 × 13-inch casserole dish with nonstick cooking spray.

In a medium saucepan set over low heat, melt ¼ cup of the butter. Add the flour and cook, whisking constantly, for 1 minute (you are basically making a roux, but you do not want it to brown). Gradually whisk in the stock until smooth. Add the nutmeg and season to taste with salt and pepper. Cook until the mixture has thickened to a creamy consistency, 10 to 12 minutes. Set aside.

In a large saucepan set over medium heat, heat the remaining ¼ cup butter and the oil. Add the shallot and green beans and cook until the beans turn bright green, 10 minutes. Add the garlic and mushrooms and cook, stirring, until the beans are crisp-tender, 15 minutes. Add the sherry and cook until it has evaporated, 5 minutes. Remove the pan from the heat. Add the reserved sauce, stir well, and pour the mixture into the prepared casserole dish.

Bake until bubbly and starting to brown, 20 to 25 minutes.

CREAMY LEEKS *in* MORNAY SAUCE

SERVES 4

Leeks are an underrated vegetable that a small minority are completely addicted to. I am one of those people (as is Amber Izzard—more about her on the opposite page). This recipe pairs leeks with good wine, better cheese, and panko bread crumbs for crunch. It is like vegetable-based macaroni and cheese, except a thousand times more sophisticated.

LEEKS

¼ cup (½ stick) unsalted butter

1 bunch leeks (white parts only), well rinsed and cut into 1-inch-thick slices (6 cups)

Salt and freshly ground black pepper

¼ cup Madeira

¼ cup dry white wine

2 cups Chicken Stock, homemade (page 45), or store-bought

MORNAY SAUCE

¼ cup (½ stick) unsalted butter

¼ cup all-purpose flour

Dash of ground nutmeg

Salt

¼ pound Gruyère cheese, shredded (1 cup)

½ cup panko bread crumbs

For the leeks, in a saucepan set over medium heat, melt the butter. Add the leeks, season with salt and pepper, and cook, stirring, until the leeks are soft and translucent, 10 minutes. Add the Madeira and cook until it has evaporated, 5 minutes. Add the white wine and cook until it has evaporated, 5 minutes. Add the stock and cook until it starts to bubble, about 10 minutes. Transfer the leeks to a bowl and reserve the liquid.

For the Mornay sauce, in a clean saucepan set over medium heat, melt the butter. Whisk in the flour and cook for 1 minute. Gradually whisk in 2 cups of the reserved liquid from cooking the leeks, and then add the nutmeg and salt to taste. Cook, stirring, until the sauce starts to bubble and thicken, 13 minutes.

Preheat the broiler. Spray a broiler-safe 8 × 8-inch baking dish with nonstick cooking spray.

Pour 2 cups of the sauce into the bowl of leeks. Add ¾ cup of the cheese and stir well. Pour into the prepared baking dish and sprinkle the remaining ¼ cup cheese and the bread crumbs over the top.

Broil until the top is golden brown, 10 minutes.

Let There Be Leeks: Brother Ken and Co.

ONCE UPON A TIME, a Baptist missionary, his wife, and his two daughters lived in Water Valley. They were righteous and godly and wonderful and spread joy and peace wherever they went. Then the two daughters went to college down in Jackson and the parents moved to Siberia.

True story.

Mr. Ken, the preacher in the family, is someone I have yet to discuss religion or politics with. We always got hung up on food: That man has a thousand different ways to cook all kinds of vegetables, gleaned from his missionary days in Togo and Ukraine. I've never seen someone get so excited about produce, other than me and Dixie.

(He also really digs Cora's fried pies.)

When we opened the B.T.C., I spent a weekend driving to a small country store in nowheresville, Tennessee, and I spent five hundred dollars on a hunk of gleaming metal that was purported to slice deli meats and cheeses. I got completely ripped off. The slicer was a thousand years old, dull as a hoe, and lacking the most basic safety precautions—yet we used it for a solid year. I didn't know much about deli equipment, so I had no incentive to upgrade.

BREAKFAST 8AM-10:30AM

Daily:
- Sausage Biscuit - $2
- Sausage & cheese Biscuit - $2.50
- Bacon, egg, & Hoop cheese Biscuit - $3
- Delta Grind Grits with Bacon or Sausage - $3.99
- two Biscuits with Sausage gravy - $4.99
- two eggs, Bacon/sausage, sourdough toast/biscuit, grits - $5.99
- The Famous Amos - Biscuit & gravy, with eggs on top & Sausage/Bacon - $6.99
- The Clifford - Fried egg & mayo Sourdough toast Sandwich - $2.99

Weekends Only
- Everything above & ...
- Pancakes, Bacon/Sausage - $4.99
- Sides - Grits, toast, Biscuit, Bacon, eggs, Sausage - $1.50
- orange juice, local milk, coffee - $1.50

Mr. Ken saw the slabs of meat we were mangling and made me an offer I couldn't refuse: a free slicer. One with a guard and an angled blade.

I said yes.

For the next year, Mr. Ken came in whenever the slicer needed assistance. He put a new blade on it, jiggled the wiring, messed with the guard, sharpened the blade. He made a thousand adjustments and never acted like I owed him anything. When I thanked him, he'd just smile at me and say, "We're glad you're here." Then he'd buy three or so quarts of yogurt. He and Miz Izzard love yogurt.

So when his daughter Amber, a junior in high school at the time, applied for a job, I was inclined to say yes.

Boy, was *that* a good decision. Amber has a mop of curly dark hair, an infectious smile, a gift for talking to people, an appreciation for good food (everything from fine cheese to asparagus to imported exotic rice), and a work ethic that blows most adults out of the water. She worked at the B.T.C. for fourteen months before she went to college, and she knows there's always a summer job waiting for her behind the copper counter. (Unfortunately for the B.T.C., she's spending her summers helping orphans in Thailand. Really.)

We changed our lunch menu recently—dropped a few items, added a few more—just to keep it interesting. Since we've opened the cafe, we've gone from being strictly a blue-collar, local kind of joint to occasionally having folks "from away" coming to lunch with us, so Dixie felt like we should add some destination salads and sandwiches as well as the hoop cheese and bologna.

This meant several things: We have to keep arugula in the kitchen at all times, for one, and also we had to find out Amber's schedule, because no one else in the world could ever letter our chalkboard menu like she does. We bought her some new bistro chalk markers, left her the instructions, and came in Monday morning to a brand-new menu, along with a note, thanking us for allowing her to spend five hours of her time repainting and lettering the menu.

Nope, she wasn't being sarcastic. She said she missed the B.T.C. down in Jackson, and it'd been nice to be back in the store for a while. She also said she was excited to see we were carrying leeks again. Amber loves leeks.

See why I think she's a winner?

YELLOW SQUASH
Au Gratin

SERVES 6

¼ cup (½ stick) plus 1 tablespoon
unsalted butter

6 to 8 small yellow squash, sliced
(4 cups)

4 eggs, beaten

2 dashes Tabasco sauce

½ teaspoon sugar

1 teaspoon salt

½ teaspoon freshly ground black
pepper

1 tablespoon extra-virgin olive oil

1 teaspoon dried basil

½ teaspoon white pepper

1 cup panko bread crumbs

2 ounces Swiss cheese, shredded
(½ cup)

2 ounces Cheddar cheese,
shredded (½ cup)

I wish I could sell you Sam Goodwin's squash for this recipe. Sam is a native Water Vallian who seems to be related to half my customers, and he also runs the local pest control company. He never wants to talk to me about bugs, though. Instead, he is a true gardener and forager. I have learned to buy whatever he brings me, which has ranged from pawpaws that have dropped from wild trees along riverbanks, to perfectly plump figs, to pearlescent yellow squash that he picks at dawn and sells to me by breakfast.

I don't even bother making a place for his squash in our produce cooler. I just set it in a bowl, situated on a blue cloth so that the yellow shines, right on the corner of the copper front counter.

It's gone by lunch.

This gratin combines perfect squash with cheese and crunchy bread crumbs. It is a crowd-pleaser and a wonderful side for, say, Cliff's Chandeleur Islands Speckled Trout (page 169). It can also carry as a vegetarian main, if you're looking for a lighter supper.

Preheat the oven to 375°F.

In a medium bowl, melt ¼ cup of the butter. Add the squash, eggs, Tabasco, sugar, ½ teaspoon of the salt, and black pepper.

In a sauté pan set over medium heat, add the oil and the remaining 1 tablespoon butter. Heat until bubbly. Add the squash mixture, ½ teaspoon remaining salt, basil, and white pepper. Cook until the squash is soft, 15 minutes. Drain well and set aside.

Put half of the squash mixture in the bottom of an 8 × 8-inch casserole dish. Sprinkle with half of the bread crumbs and then half of each of the cheeses. Repeat the layers with the remaining ingredients.

Bake until golden brown on top, 15 minutes.

BAKED SQUASH
with Vidalia Onions

SERVES 4

I have met a handful of people in my life whose souls are so incandescent they humble everyone in their vicinity. Junior Cook is one of those folks. And in addition to being a sweet soul. Mr. Cook has probably the prettiest garden in town. It is a place of wonder and simplicity: a fenced-in plot with neat cages of tomatoes, trellised beans, hills of squash, and a big blue rain barrel that he keeps manure in to feed his tomatoes. Seeing as Mr. and Mrs. Cook live alone and have a bountiful garden, I had the thought to ask Mr. Cook if he'd sell me some of his extra produce.

I ran into him at the bank as he exited his immaculate, decades-old red and white Ford pickup truck and said, "Mr. Cook, howsabout if you have any extra tomatoes or squash on your hands, you come down to the store and I'll give you a fair price on them?"

He shook his head. "No, ma'am," he said. "The missus and I decided a long time ago that as long as the Lord would bless us with enough to eat, we wouldn't sell the extra. We just give it away."

Hard to argue with that. If you have someone in your life who leaves plastic bags full of freshly picked squash or sweet onions on your porch, make this recipe. It is savory enough to pair with just about anything for a meat-and-three kind of dinner, or you could just have it as your main and make a simple salad, like Cucumber Tomato Salad (page 88), to accompany it.

¼ cup (½ stick) unsalted butter

2 tablespoons extra-virgin olive oil

1 large Vidalia onion, thinly sliced

2 pounds yellow squash, sliced (8 cups)

½ pound Swiss cheese, shredded (1½ cups)

1 garlic clove, chopped

1 cup heavy cream

2 tablespoons sour cream

1 tablespoon dry vermouth

1 tablespoon Worcestershire sauce

2 eggs, beaten

1 tablespoon chopped fresh tarragon

1 tablespoon chopped fresh chives

1 tablespoon dried basil

½ teaspoon freshly ground black pepper

⅛ teaspoon crushed red pepper flakes

1 cup panko bread crumbs

Preheat the oven to 375°F. Spray a 9 × 13-inch baking dish with nonstick cooking spray.

In a large skillet set over medium heat, heat the butter and oil. Add the onion and cook, stirring, until soft, 5 minutes. Add the squash and cook until soft, 10 minutes. Remove the pan from the heat and add the cheese, garlic, cream, sour cream, vermouth, Worcestershire sauce, eggs, tarragon, chives, basil, black pepper, and red pepper flakes. Pour the mixture into the prepared baking dish and sprinkle the bread crumbs over the top.

Bake until the bread crumbs are golden brown, 25 minutes.

CRABMEAT-
STUFFED *Mushrooms*

SERVES 4

I'm not going to lie. I have a few—a very few, I promise—customers I smile at only because their shopping buggies are full. The one I'm fixing to tell you about I really did like, even though he upped and moved to California and I haven't seen him in a while.

He was a young good-looking guy, small and skinny, who was always moving fast and refilling his travel coffee mug. He raised chickens, worked as an archaeologist field researcher, and occasionally sported overalls. He liked pork chops, strong coffee, and locally grown vegetables. He told me all about his plans to raise his own mushrooms: the location, the setup, even the strength of the lighting, for heaven's sake.

(This happens all the time. I had another fellow whip out his cell phone the other day to show me pictures of his tomatoes that he managed to ripen in February.)

Anyhow. I never did get any of those mushrooms, though I promised to buy some if they made it to harvest.

If you do grow or procure some beautiful plain ole button mushrooms, this is a great fancy recipe for them. I think they're awesome as a side, and they make a nice hors d'oeuvre, too.

½ cup (1 stick) unsalted butter

6 green onions, finely chopped

1 pound jumbo lump crabmeat, shells and cartilage discarded

1 cup panko bread crumbs

2 tablespoons chopped fresh chives

2 tablespoons chopped fresh tarragon

1 teaspoon Old Bay seasoning

1 teaspoon freshly ground black pepper

Dash of Tabasco sauce

3 eggs, beaten

12 large button mushroom caps

¼ cup grated Parmesan cheese

Preheat the oven to 375°F. Melt ¼ cup of the butter and put it in the bottom of an 8 × 8-inch baking dish.

In a sauté pan set over medium heat, melt the remaining ¼ cup butter. Add the onions and cook, stirring, for 1 minute. Add the crabmeat, bread crumbs, chives, tarragon, Old Bay, pepper, and Tabasco and cook, stirring, until the bread crumbs brown a little, about 2 minutes. Reduce the heat to low and stir in the eggs (be careful not to scramble the eggs). Remove the pan from the heat.

Stuff the mushroom caps with the mixture and put them in the prepared baking dish. Sprinkle the tops with the cheese.

Bake until the tops are golden brown, 20 minutes.

Oh, That's Just . . .
an Ode to the Long Memories and
Big Hearts of Small Towns

BEFORE MOVING to Water Valley, I'd never lived in a small town. I'd grown up on seventy acres in Virginia horse country, where antebellum homes dotted the landscape and imported autos cruised the twisting blacktop roads. My sister and I would gauge how prosperous a farm was by the number of boards their fence used: three boards was passing, but the crossed fences with the top and bottom rail—a total of five boards—was for the really well-off, the people who could spend tens of thousands of dollars on their weekend or retirement home's edging. It can be a lonely place. Water Valley doesn't have so many imported autos and it's impossible to drive down any street anywhere without bumping into someone who wants to talk to you. Here, it's hard to be lonely.

People have spoken a lot about the rigid nature of small towns, but what I've experienced has been quite the opposite. There is a tolerance for peccadillos here: The local vet, for instance, is an avid hunter, takes off for two weeks every fall to go hunting, and his veterinary office is festooned with the taxidermic remains of his trophies. Seriously, there is a *ton* of dead animals on that man's pine-paneled walls.

After a few years, it stopped being weird.

So one day, shortly after my move here, I was listening to an elderly lady tell me about life in Water Valley, and she got to discoursing on her feelings about prescription medication. She very matter-of-factly told me that years ago, a local physician had become addicted to prescription meds and ended up losing his license over the whole shebang before going to rehab.

I found the story mildly astonishing, but what really knocked my socks off was the end of the story: namely, that his life in the town did not end there. The good doctor went to rehab, won back his medical license, and returned to practice. He also began to serve the community in a new way, by being an active and founding board member of the local rehabilitation unit that helps so many in our small town.

Small towns may know all your secrets, but they also know you. They witness your falls and your redemptions. No one's missteps are ever forgotten, but then neither are your youth and your triumphs. Heady stuff, to be known so fully.

ROOT VEGETABLE MASH

SERVES 6

Summer produce is the sexy stuff. Heirloom tomatoes, purple basil, baskets filled with squashes and zucchinis, melons that groan and split at the touch of a knife. But root vegetables are the sturdy handmaidens of winter. They surprise you with their sheer goodness, so give them a chance and immerse yourself in the earthy sweetness of potatoes, turnips, parsnips, and ruta-bagas. This dish is sweet, comforting, and flavorful, and pairs wonderfully with Roasted Pork Tenderloin with Apricot–Apple Cider Glaze (page 159).

2 medium Yukon gold potatoes, peeled and chopped (1 cup)

1 small turnip, peeled and chopped (1 cup)

4 small parsnips, peeled and chopped (1 cup)

2 medium carrots, chopped (1 cup)

½ large rutabaga, peeled and chopped (1 cup)

1 tablespoon plus 1 teaspoon kosher salt

½ cup heavy cream

½ cup (1 stick) unsalted butter

¼ cup sour cream

¼ teaspoon freshly ground black pepper

Put the potatoes, turnip, parsnips, carrots, rutabaga, and 1 tablespoon of the salt in a 6-quart pot. Cover with water, set over high heat, and bring to a boil. Cook until the vegetables are fork-tender, 15 to 20 minutes.

Meanwhile, in a separate saucepan set over medium heat, combine the cream and butter and heat until just warm, 5 minutes. Turn off the heat and keep the pan on the stove.

When the vegetables are done, drain them well and return them to the warm pot. Add the warm cream and butter mixture and mash with a handheld potato masher until the desired consistency. Add the sour cream, remaining 1 teaspoon salt, and the pepper. Serve immediately.

CLIFF'S HOMINY SAN JUAN

SERVES 4

2 (16-ounce) cans of hominy (one white, one golden, if available), drained

¼ pound sharp Cheddar cheese, shredded (1 cup)

1 (4-ounce) can chopped mild green chile peppers

1 cup sour cream

Salt

Sweet paprika, for garnish

Variations

HOMINY SAN NICOLAS (CHRISTMAS): Garnish with chopped green and red bell peppers.

HOPPITY SAN JUAN (EASTER): Garnish with mini-marshmallows.

HOMINY SAN WASHINGTON: Garnish with bacon bits.

Cliff (see page 169) also makes this indescribable but delicious dish that hails from his bachelor days. He actually went to Harvard Law School but never practiced. Nowadays, he rents a small office above the B.T.C. where he works on his novel sometimes and, more often, on his federally funded history of a military fort in Bakersfield, California. His door reads CLIFF LAWSON, WRITER in gold leaf.

To make a sizable potluck-size serving, quadruple the hominy, triple the other ingredients, and cook for 3 hours.

In the bowl of a slow cooker, such as a Crock-Pot, combine the hominy, cheese, chiles, and sour cream. Cook on low for 2 hours, stirring occasionally.

Season with salt to taste. Sprinkle each serving with paprika.

FETACHOKE CUPS

MAKES 48 MINI-CUPS

Paoli Banchetti lives an hour's drive from the B.T.C., but she makes the drive shockingly often to eat lunch and spend some time perusing the store. Paoli comes from good Italian stock and cooks voraciously and well.

This particular recipe is something Paoli cobbled together from a pecan tassie crust recipe and a dip from the well-known local cook Mrs. Leet of Indianola, whom Paoli knew as a child.

For the crust, in a medium bowl, blend the butter and cream cheese with a rubber spatula. Add the flour and mix well. Shape the mixture into a disc that's about 1 inch thick. Wrap in parchment paper or plastic wrap and refrigerate for at least 30 minutes.

Meanwhile, *for the filling,* in a medium bowl, combine the artichokes, onions, tomatoes, cheeses, mayonnaise, lemon juice, pepper, and Cavender's seasoning. Cover the bowl and refrigerate for at least 30 minutes or until ready to use.

Preheat the oven to 375°F.

Break off a 2-inch piece of dough, roll it into a ball, and press it into a circle. Press the dough into a cup of a mini-muffin pan, letting the dough come up over the rim of the cup. Put a heaping tablespoon of filling in the center of the dough; repeat with the remaining ingredients.

Bake until the crust is golden brown, 27 minutes. Carefully take them out of the pan one by one and let cool on a wire rack (do not turn upside down) for 15 minutes before serving.

They will keep in an airtight container in the refrigerator for 4 days.

PIE CRUST

1 cup (2 sticks) unsalted butter, room temperature

1 (6-ounce) package cream cheese, room temperature

2 cups all-purpose flour

FILLING

1 (14.5-ounce) can artichoke hearts, drained and finely chopped

½ cup finely chopped green onions

½ cup finely chopped tomatoes

½ cup grated Parmesan cheese

¼ pound feta cheese, crumbled

1 cup Hellmann's mayonnaise

2 tablespoons fresh lemon juice

1 teaspoon freshly ground black pepper

½ teaspoon Cavender's Greek seasoning

CORN BREAD DRESSING

SERVES 8

¼ cup (½ stick) unsalted butter

1 small yellow onion, finely chopped

4 celery hearts (with leaves), finely chopped

1 small green bell pepper, cored, seeded, and grated

Dixie's Corn Bread (recipe follows), crumbled

6 to 8 cups Chicken Stock, homemade (page 45) or store-bought

1 (10-ounce) can cream of chicken soup

4 large eggs, lightly beaten

Dash of Tabasco sauce

1 heaping tablespoon dried sage

1 teaspoon salt

½ teaspoon freshly ground black pepper

Note

Once you've put the dressing in the casserole dish, you can cover and refrigerate it for up to 2 days. This is what Dixie does, so that she can be plenty prepared for the holidays. Then you just need to take it out and bake it the day of your feast.

First of all, understand this: There is no stuffing in the South. No herbed or chestnut or oyster-flavored bread crumbs. There is only corn bread dressing. And for many, corn bread dressing *is* the holiday meal.

It is the first thing people scoop onto their plates. And in case the South is ever again invaded, Dixie swears that this will be what you'll hear in house after house: "Grab the silver and the dressing recipe and bury it in the backyard!"

Good corn bread dressing starts with good corn bread and finishes with giblet gravy. And never does it ever touch the inside of a bird.

Preheat the oven to 400°F. Spray a 9 × 13-inch baking dish with nonstick cooking spray.

In a large skillet set over medium heat, melt the butter. Add the onion, celery, and bell pepper and cook, stirring, until soft, 10 minutes. Remove the pan from the heat and let cool for 20 minutes.

In a large bowl, combine the cooked vegetables, corn bread, 6 cups of the stock, soup, eggs, Tabasco, sage, salt, and pepper. Mix well. You may have to add a little more stock; you want the mixture to be wet but not soupy. Pour the dressing into the prepared baking dish.

Bake until golden brown on top and with a slight jiggle in the center, or until a wooden toothpick inserted in the center comes out clean, 30 to 45 minutes. Be careful to not overbake. Let the dressing sit for 1 hour before serving.

DIXIE'S CORN BREAD

SERVES 6

Put a 12-inch cast-iron skillet in the oven and preheat the oven to 425°F.

In a small bowl, whisk together the cornmeal, flour, baking powder, baking soda, and salt.

In a separate bowl, whisk together the buttermilk, eggs, bacon grease, and butter. Slowly whisk the dry ingredients into the wet ingredients until just mixed with no lumps (do not overmix). Carefully remove the skillet from the oven and pour in the corn bread batter.

Bake until a wooden toothpick inserted in the center comes out clean, 20 to 30 minutes.

2 cups cornmeal

½ cup all-purpose flour

2 teaspoons baking powder

½ teaspoon baking soda

½ teaspoon salt

1½ cups buttermilk

2 eggs, beaten

4 tablespoons bacon grease

2 tablespoons unsalted butter, melted

Note

Dixie always has some bacon grease around, and it's her secret weapon for getting a nice, crisp crust on her corn bread. When she pulls the hot skillet out of the oven, she dips a paper towel in the grease and quickly rubs the inside of the skillet before pouring in the batter.

Perfect WHITE RICE

SERVES 2

1 cup long-grain white rice

1 teaspoon unsalted butter

1 teaspoon kosher salt

Sometimes the simplest things are the hardest to perfect. Rice is one of those things. In my pre-Dixie days, I used to just boil it like pasta and drain. It wasn't very fluffy, but at least the rice wasn't stuck to the bottom of the pot either. Luckily for all of us, Dixie is in our lives, and here is her recipe for foolproof white rice.

In a medium pot with a tight-fitting lid, combine 1¾ cups of water, the rice, butter, and salt. Bring to a boil over high heat. Decrease the heat to low and cover. Cook at a gentle simmer until the water is completely absorbed and the rice is tender, about 12 minutes.

Remove the pot from the heat and let it sit, undisturbed with the lid on, for at least 5 minutes and for as long as 30 minutes. Remove the lid, fluff the rice gently with a fork, and serve.

The North Mississippi Herald:
The Only Publication I Anxiously Await

WHEN I MOVED TO WATER VALLEY, the local paper struck me as ludicrous. It's very thin and there's a whole page devoted to church news, for heaven's sake.

But the *Herald* has a way of winning over skeptics. For one, David and Jack—the editor and the writer, respectively—do a killer job of showcasing the shenanigans of the local politicians. You know it's going to be worth reading if there's a six-thousand-word article devoted entirely to quotes: what alderman said what on some crazy, you-never-would-have-believed-it issue. I think the newspaper helps keep our town government accountable, and that's always a good thing.

For another, it's quirky. I was reading the classifieds one day. The lost-and-found section consisted of the following: "Lost: pair of dentures on Clay Street; reward! Found: red goat. Very docile."

And then there's Betty's Week, a column written by Miss Betty, who has penned a weekly account of her life for decades. The B.T.C. has been profiled in the Oxford papers, some local magazines, the *New York Times*, the *Wall Street Journal*, and *Food & Wine* magazine, but none has made me as happy as that week Betty told the world she'd bought peaches at my store.

Plus, there's the matter of when I was a new kid in town, the *Herald* paid me to go from person to person and sit down and talk to folks about their lives. As well as being a confidence booster (at the time, I was both childless and jobless, which was . . . unnerving), it was also the best introduction to Water Valley I could have wished for. All in all, I interviewed more than fifty folks and learned firsthand about hobbies like James Tribble's exotic

pheasant raising to history's like Mr. Wade's World War II experience to—everything. I actually sat down with Mr. Parker, who ran a legendary five-and-dime store for decades in what is now the B.T.C., way before Kagan and I ever thought of buying his old building, and heard about how Mr. Paul had done everything from helping a black friend escape a mob to starting a small business in Water Valley in the 1930s to turning down a partnership with Sam Walton.

People have amazing lives.

Southern Sweet Thangs

FRIED PIES

SWEET POTATO PIE
with ROSEMARY CRUST

KEY LIME PIE

PEACH ICEBOX PIE

CHESS PIE

CHARLIE BROWN COOKIES

MRS. JO'S BANANA PUDDING

PEACH POUND CAKE

LEMON POUND CAKE

TEA CAKES

SWEET AUTUMN CAKE

CHOCOLATE BUTTERMILK CAKE

LANE CAKE

STEEL MAGNOLIA CAKE

FRIED PIES

MAKES 10 PIES (OR 2 9-INCH PIES)

The odds are good that if you drive down Water Valley's Main Street on any given morning, Cora's sandwich board, a homemade affair, will be propped up in front of the store advertising warm fried pies. The odds are also good that someone will be walking out of the store holding one that's been wrapped in wax paper and tied with a pink ribbon.

Fried pies are known elsewhere in the country as hand pies. Here in Mississippi, they're as common as whoopee pies are up north; you'll find them at farmers' markets, gas stations, and of course, the B.T.C. Cora actually bakes hers, a practice that sets many an old-timer nodding and saying that's how his or her mother did it. She skips the grease in favor of a flaky just-sweet-enough treat that's ideal for a decadent breakfast or an afternoon pick-me-up.

Feel free to experiment with the fillings. Cora regularly bakes apple, peach, blueberry, pecan, sweet potato, and chocolate, but down in New Orleans, there's a fried pie shop called Hubig's that goes as far as pineapple, coconut, and banana.

CRUST

2 cups all-purpose flour

1 teaspoon salt

1 cup (2 sticks) unsalted butter, cold

¼ cup ice water

1 tablespoon raw sugar

2 recipes of your pie filling of choice (recipes follow)

Preheat the oven to 350°F. Spray a baking sheet with nonstick cooking spray.

In a large bowl, combine the flour and salt. Cut in ¾ cup (1½ sticks) of the butter with a pastry cutter or fork until the mixture is crumbly. Add the water a little at a time and stir until it comes together in a ball. Transfer the dough to a floured surface and roll it out until it is about ⅛ inch thick. Using a glass or saucer, depending on how big you want the pie (Cora uses a plastic lid that's about 6 inches in diameter), cut out circles of dough. Spoon about 3 tablespoons of the filling on one side of the circle, about ½ inch from the edge. Fold over the opposite side to make a half circle. Press the edges together with a fork to seal. Put the pies on the prepared baking sheet. Melt the remaining ¼ cup (½ stick) butter and brush the pies with it (a paint brush, pastry brush, or even a paper towel dipped in butter will work). Sprinkle with the sugar.

Bake until golden brown, 20 minutes. Transfer the pies to a wire rack and let cool.

FRIED PIE FILLINGS

I've included a few of our greatest hits here, but any sort of pie filling can be adapted for fried pies. You can even combine different fillings for other flavors. One of Cora's knockout combos is Caramel Apple; just add a little of each of the apple filling and caramel filling, and there you go.

EACH RECIPE MAKES ENOUGH FOR 5 FRIED PIES

APPLE

3 pounds Granny Smith apples

½ cup sugar

⅓ cup apple juice

3 tablespoons unsalted butter

2 teaspoons ground cinnamon, or to taste

Peel, core, and chop the apples and put them in a medium saucepan. Add the sugar and apple juice. Put the saucepan over medium heat and cook until the apples are just turning soft, 10 to 12 minutes. Remove the pan from the heat, add the butter and cinnamon, and stir well. Let cool completely before using.

CHOCOLATE

1 cup sugar

½ cup unsweetened cocoa powder

3 tablespoons cornstarch

1 tablespoon all-purpose flour

2½ cups whole milk

3 egg yolks, beaten

1 teaspoon vanilla extract

In a medium saucepan, combine the sugar, cocoa powder, cornstarch, and flour.

In a small saucepan set over medium heat, heat the milk until steaming but not boiling, 5 to 7 minutes. While stirring constantly, gradually add the hot milk to the sugar mixture. Set the pan over medium-high heat and cook, stirring constantly, until steaming but not boiling, 5 minutes. While whisking vigorously, very slowly add the egg yolks to the chocolate and cook until thickened, 2 to 3 minutes. Remove the pan from the heat and add the vanilla. Pour the mixture into a bowl and put plastic wrap directly on the surface of the filling to prevent a film from forming. Put the bowl in the refrigerator and let the filling cool completely before using.

PEACH

8 medium peaches, peeled,
   pitted, and sliced (4 cups)

¼ cup packed light brown sugar

2 tablespoons unsalted butter

½ teaspoon ground cinnamon

Dash of ground cloves

Put the peaches in a medium saucepan, and add the brown sugar. Set the saucepan over medium heat and cook, stirring, until heated through, 10 minutes. Add the butter, cinnamon, and cloves, and stir well. Remove the pan from the heat and let the filling cool completely before using.

BUTTERMILK

½ cup (1 stick) unsalted butter

½ cup buttermilk

3 eggs, beaten

1 teaspoon vanilla extract

1½ cups sugar

1 tablespoon all-purpose flour

1 tablespoon cornstarch

In a medium saucepan set over medium-high heat, melt the butter. Add the buttermilk, eggs, vanilla, sugar, flour, and cornstarch. Cook, stirring, until the mixture has thickened, 10 to 12 minutes. Remove the pan from the heat, and let the filling cool completely before using.

CARAMEL

1½ cups whole milk

¼ cup (½ stick) unsalted butter

3 egg yolks, beaten

1¼ cups sugar

2 tablespoons all-purpose flour

Dash of salt

1 teaspoon vanilla extract

In a medium saucepan set over medium-high heat, combine the milk, butter, egg yolks, ¾ cup of the sugar, the flour, and salt. Bring the mixture to a boil, stirring constantly so that it doesn't burn, about 5 minutes. Keep the mixture at a boil, stirring with one hand while you proceed.

Put the remaining ½ cup sugar in a cast-iron skillet. Set it over medium-high heat and cook the sugar, stirring constantly with a wooden spoon, until it melts, turns brown, and is completely dissolved, about 8 minutes. Take 2 tablespoons of the boiling milk mixture and add it to the dissolved sugar. Stir constantly with a whisk for about 5 seconds, and then, while whisking constantly, slowly pour the sugar mixture into the boiling milk mixture. Continue to whisk the mixture until it thickens, about 4 minutes. Remove the pan from the heat and add the vanilla. Let cool completely before using.

SWEET POTATO
PIE *with Rosemary Crust*

SERVES 8

Recently, a local farmer whose wife loves kale and gourmet ice cream started selling me sweet potatoes. This is delightful for several reasons: One, it brings his supernice wife in the store more often, and the odds are good she'll walk out with a pint of some flavor of Sweet Magnolia—the kind of ice cream we stock. The second reason is that Mr. Williamson's sweet potatoes are beautiful. I adore beautiful vegetables. They're easier to sell, and plus, they get my heart pounding.

Another reason I'm delighted is that being buddies with Mr. Williamson means that if he finds an odd-looking sweet potato in the field, he'll bring it in and make a show out of it. There's one on the counter right now that looks like a Tim Burton creation. We at the B.T.C. call these "inspiration vegetables." (Ask Dixie sometime about the carrot named Lola.)

Before moving to Mississippi, my acquaintance with the sweet potato was solely healthful, that is, wrapped in foil and baked. But folks down here don't eat pumpkin pie for Thanksgiving. They eat sweet potato pie instead. This particular version is absolutely phenomenal and has made grown calorie-counting women lick their fingers and reach for another piece.

Preheat the oven to 375°. Do *not* grease your 9-inch pie dish.

For the crust, in a large bowl, combine the flour, cornmeal, sugar, and rosemary. Cut in the butter using a pastry cutter or a fork until the mixture is crumbly. Add ice water a little at a time until the dough is moist and comes together in a ball. Put the dough on a floured work surface and knead it until it's no longer sticky, about 8 minutes. Roll out the dough into a 10-inch circle and put it in the pie dish.

For the filling, combine the sweet potatoes, sugar, butter, sweetened condensed milk, vanilla, cinnamon, and allspice in a large bowl. Pour into the pie crust.

Bake until firm, 20 to 30 minutes. The pie can be served warm or at room temperature.

ROSEMARY CRUST

1 cup all-purpose flour

½ cup cornmeal

¼ cup confectioners' sugar

3 teaspoons chopped fresh rosemary

½ cup (1 stick) unsalted butter, cold and cut into pieces

¼ cup ice water

FILLING

2 cups mashed cooked sweet potatoes

1½ cups sugar

½ cup (1 stick) unsalted butter, melted

1 (8-ounce) can sweetened condensed milk

1 teaspoon vanilla extract

¼ teaspoon ground cinnamon

¼ teaspoon ground allspice

Mississippi: A Long, Slow Seduction

I HAVE A LOT OF JET-SETTERS in my life. Cousins in New York City; my sister in Washington, DC; Kagan's best friend in Los Angeles—these folks frequently travel, for work and pleasure, to places you see in travel magazines: the Virgin Islands, Lake Tahoe, the English Thames. (I have a cousin who rows crew internationally.) My father lives in Charlottesville, Virginia; my mother lives adjacent to a national park so beautiful that tourists from all over the world come to gawk; and Kagan's older sister lives in the shadow of a white-capped mountain with waterfalls and all in the glory that is Vermont.

My corner of Mississippi can be a tough sell to the uninitiated eye. There are trailers, roadside trash, abandoned buildings, stray dogs, bizarre and antiquated alcohol laws, a propensity to ask what church you belong to, lumbering of the slash-and-burn variety, and a comfort with irregular business hours. It's an hour's drive to a mall, and if you're not an eighteen-year-old girl with sorority-girl style, shopping options are limited.

But if I started to list the virtues of this wonderful wild corner of the world, I could go on for days. It takes a little while for the slow seductiveness of this Mississippi small town to sink in: This isn't in-your-face beauty but rather a wholesomeness that grows more and more attractive with time. It's arched pecan trees over green glades, daffodils in January, sweetgum balls that Caspian presents to me as a gift. Small-town Mississippi is a place where our kids ride bikes down sidewalks and all the storekeepers know their names; a place where they will someday cut through the woods to play with their peers; a place where waitresses, rock stars, sandwich makers, and professors are all friends and neighbors.

It's not glitzy, this adopted state of mine. But it's like all things good: better in the actuality than in the idea.

KEY LIME PIE

SERVES 8

Whenever folks mention bachelor parties, I make Kagan tell everybody about his.

My husband is six foot six, but he can't drink more than two beers without it going to his head. In the porch-swinging, tailgating, hard-drinking Deep South, this makes him (and me, because I'm the same way) slightly suspect. After first meeting us, Coulter told her music-producer rock-star-managing husband, Amos, "But they don't *drink*."

Kagan also has a deep and fundamental abhorrence of loose women (must be the New England Puritan in him). So when he proposed a bachelor party before we were married, I was a little curious as to what he'd come up with.

Here's what happened: He and his childhood best friend, Nicholas (who lives on the West Coast and makes completely, utterly, deeply fabulous pies with his wife, Emily, at I Heart Pies: check 'em out), decided to go somewhere warm, somewhere sunny, somewhere they could go snorkeling.

So they flew to Key West. Just the two of them. They checked into a bed-and-breakfast and spent a night getting snockered in a hot tub. Every time Cora makes her tart and delicious key lime pies, I think about my husband, cluelessly wandering Florida's homosexual haven with his best friend, and it makes me giggle.

This particular key lime pie is extra limey. She made it as a dessert special the other day, and reactions ran the gamut from "Please give me the recipe" to "That was the best pie I ever ate" to "Way too much lime for me." So save this one for the people in your life who adore key lime pie.

1 (8-ounce) can sweetened condensed milk

½ cup bottled key lime juice (Cora uses Real Lime brand)

3 egg yolks

2 drops green food coloring

1 (9-inch) store-bought graham cracker crust

Preheat the oven to 325°F.

In a large bowl, combine the sweetened condensed milk, lime juice, egg yolks, and food coloring. Pour into the crust.

Bake until the middle is set, about 40 minutes. Let cool completely before serving.

PEACH ICEBOX PIE

CRUST

1 (11-ounce) box vanilla wafers (Dixie prefers Jackson's brand)

¼ cup confectioners' sugar

¾ cup (1½ sticks) unsalted butter, melted

FILLING

1 (8-ounce) can sweetened condensed milk

Juice of 2 lemons

4 medium peaches, peeled, pitted, and sliced (2 cups)

SERVES 8

Icebox pie is for the dog days of summer. I don't understand how folks lived in Mississippi without air-conditioning, and I grew up without air-conditioning. Mississippi is a whole 'nother level of hot. Icebox pie is a perfect dessert for this time of year: easy, no-fuss, and no-bake, so everyone can have dessert without anyone having to turn on the oven.

We have a lot of relatives in the North who question our location solely on the basis of summer. Well, sure. Summer can be nasty. But it's like winter in Vermont: you just keep your head down and scuttle between car and house as fast as you can.

Also, we tend to visit said relatives in the North during the summer.

The folks I really wonder about are the Amish farmers in Randolph, Mississippi. Everybody is wearing dark cloth from head to toe, and they sleep without so much as a fan in tin-roofed farmhouses with shade trees that aren't yet tall enough to arch over the house (the settlement is about ten years old). Maybe everybody sleeps in the basement. They do have nice basements, all of them built to the same plan, with a long bench meant to hold pickled goods, and also handy if anybody wanted to take a nap in the cool air.

If it's too hot to turn on the oven, icebox pie is the way to go. This one is a nice change from the classic lemon and is a fantastic way to employ summertime's greatest fruit, the fresh peach.

For the crust, put half of the vanilla wafers in a food processor and pulse until you have fine crumbs. Add the sugar and pulse until blended. Add the butter a little at a time and pulse until the mixture holds together. Press the mixture into a 9-inch pie dish. Arrange the remaining whole vanilla wafers around the inside edge of the pie dish.

For the filling, in a large bowl, combine the sweetened condensed milk, lemon juice, and peaches. Pour into the crust.

Put the pie in the refrigerator and chill for at least 8 hours until set. The pie will keep in the freezer for up to 3 days.

CHESS PIE

SERVES 8

About four months after the B.T.C. opened, our baked goods provider informed me that they couldn't source any cookies or pies for us for the next two months. I thought about working in a store with no freshly baked anythings for sixty days and realized one thing very clearly: ain't no way, no how.

Then I remembered Cora.

A native Water Vallian, Cora is the daughter of Binnie and Jo Turnage, the proprietors of the drugstore down the street. She's also a talented home baker who had recently returned to her hometown and found herself at a loss for what to do.

We sat down over coffee and made each other a deal. Two years later, Cora still bakes at the B.T.C. five out of every seven days. She loads up her table with whatever tickles her fancy, and people come in and exclaim with delight because things are still warm from the oven. Cora is a Pinterest fan and magazine reader and is always trying new things, but the recipes here are the ones she makes often or always. She uses a regular stand mixer and a cheap electric stove, and every single one of her desserts turns out fabulously each time. Chess Pie is custardy, creamy, and a top seller.

3 large eggs, beaten

½ cup buttermilk

⅓ cup (⅔ stick) unsalted butter, melted

1 teaspoon vanilla extract

1½ cups sugar

1 tablespoon all-purpose flour

Dash of salt

1 (9-inch) store-bought pie shell (see Note, page 29)

Preheat the oven to 350°F.

In a medium bowl, combine the eggs, buttermilk, butter, vanilla, sugar, flour, and salt. Pour the mixture into the pie shell.

Bake until the top is golden brown and the center doesn't jiggle, about 1 hour. Let cool to room temperature before slicing.

CHARLIE BROWN COOKIES

MAKES 8 LARGE COOKIES

I asked my son, Caspian, yesterday what his favorite day in his whole life was. Caspian is three, tall for his age, with sturdy shoulders, huge brown eyes with long lashes, and short straight brown hair that shows his sticking-out ears. He loves food intensely and with abandon; he likes bugs, worms, and giving our cat Priscilla full-body hugs. (Strangely, Priscilla adores Caspian.)

He said Halloween right off the bat.

I've always thought of small towns as having an unnerving population of elderly, but Water Valley has a ton of kids growing up in it. This year for Halloween, we walked down to Tatums' house: John and Becky are about our age, and they also have two kids, a girl a little older than Annaliese, a boy the same age as Caspian.

We heard the party before we saw it: Their front porch and yard were crawling with children. Kagan and I let our children join the party and run wild. Caspian took somebody's light saber and had a sword fight with Amos Henry. Annaliese and Louisa complimented each other's costumes. We drank out of plastic cups and listened to the sounds of the children for twenty minutes or so, and then we corralled them for a group picture and started walking from house to house. It took two hours to go three blocks.

Charlie Brown cookies delight children and adults alike. Chewy yet soft and full of crowd-pleasers like cranberries and white chocolate chips, these cookies are hand-size classics that go wonderfully with a cold glass of milk.

1 cup (2 sticks) unsalted butter, room temperature

2 cups sugar

2 eggs

1 teaspoon vanilla extract

1¾ cups all-purpose flour

1 teaspoon baking soda

1 teaspoon ground cinnamon

Dash of salt

2 cups rolled oats (quick-cooking or old-fashioned will work)

1 cup chopped nuts (Cora uses pecans or walnuts)

1 cup sweetened shredded coconut

1 cup white chocolate chips

1 cup dried cranberries

Preheat the oven to 350°F. Line a baking sheet with parchment paper.

In a large bowl, cream the butter and sugar. Add the eggs and vanilla, and stir well.

In a separate bowl, combine the flour, baking soda, cinnamon, and salt. Add the flour mixture to the sugar mixture, and stir well. Add the oats, nuts, coconut, chocolate chips, and dried cranberries. Drop the batter in 3-inch mounds onto the prepared baking sheet.

Bake until firm and light brown on top, 10 to 12 minutes. Transfer the cookies to a wire rack and let cool completely.

The cookies will keep in an airtight container for 4 days.

Mrs. Jo's BANANA PUDDING

SERVES 6

1½ cups whole milk

¼ cup (½ stick) unsalted butter

2 eggs, beaten

1½ cups sugar

1 tablespoon all-purpose flour

1 teaspoon vanilla extract

¼ teaspoon fresh lemon juice

1 (11-ounce) box vanilla wafers
(Dixie prefers Jackson's brand)

3 to 4 ripe bananas, sliced

Cora's mother is Mrs. Jo, wife of Binnie, mother to five, and co-runner of Turnage Drug Store down the street. She is well known in Water Valley for being an excellent home cook.

For a while there, Mrs. Jo would make big bowls of this banana pudding—which she created by combining her mother's and her mother-in-law's recipes—and send it to the store with Cora to share. After witnessing me and Dixie scraping our spoons against bowls for a while, Cora decided to make it for a lunch dessert special and now serves it from 11 AM to 2 PM at least once a week. Mrs. Jo and Cora recommend serving this at room temperature; whipped cream on top doesn't hurt, either. It's embarrassing how much of this I can eat.

In a microwave-safe bowl, combine the milk, butter, eggs, sugar, and flour. Microwave on high for 6 to 7 minutes, stirring every 2 minutes, until creamy and fully blended. Add the vanilla and lemon juice and stir.

In a 10 × 6-inch casserole dish (Cora uses a CorningWare casserole dish), make a layer of cookies, followed by a layer of banana slices. Repeat the layers and make a final layer of cookies. Pour the pudding over the layers. Let it sit for about 10 minutes before serving.

Peach POUND CAKE

1 cup (2 sticks) unsalted butter, room temperature

½ cup Crisco shortening

3 cups sugar

6 eggs

1 (3-ounce) box peach-flavored instant gelatin

1 teaspoon vanilla extract

3½ cups all-purpose flour

¼ teaspoon baking powder

¼ teaspoon salt

1 cup buttermilk

4 medium peaches, peeled, pitted, and chopped (2 cups)

**MAKES 1 BUNDT CAKE
or 4 (4 × 7-INCH) LOAF CAKES**

Cora makes this pound cake during peach season, that magical time from May and to September when we're moving box upon box of this southern fruit in and out of the van like crazy people. We heap bushel baskets with peaches and set them on the counter, by the counter, on the fruit cart, and just about everybody who comes in the store leaves with at least a couple.

Folks swear that the peaches we sell taste better than the store-bought peaches. When they say this to me, I resist the urge to point out that we are, in fact, a store, and instead just nod. I know what they mean. But I don't stock just any peaches.

First of all, about half the time, we're selling peaches from Joey down the street at Sartain's hardware store. Joey has three hundred peach trees he manages and his peaches are perfect.

So when peach season is in full swing and I've got fifteen pounds of Tuesday's peaches left and one-hundred-plus pounds getting unloaded, I tend to take them into the kitchen and let Dixie chop 'em for a salsa, or more commonly, Cora uses them for her fried pies, lattice-topped pies, or, enchantingly, in peach pound cake.

Preheat the oven to 350°F. Spray a Bundt pan (or four 4 × 7-inch loaf pans) with nonstick cooking spray.

In the bowl of a stand mixer, cream the butter, shortening, and sugar. Add the eggs one at a time, and then add the gelatin and vanilla.

In a separate bowl, sift together the flour, baking powder, and salt. Alternately add the flour mixture and the buttermilk to the butter mixture and stir well. Stir in the peaches, and pour the batter into the prepared pan.

Bake until a wooden toothpick inserted into the center of the cake comes out clean, 1 hour. Transfer to a wire rack and let cool completely before inverting onto a serving plate.

Lemon POUND CAKE

MAKES 1 BUNDT CAKE
or **4 (4 × 7-INCH) LOAF CAKES**

My sister is named Eliza Lee van Beuren. She is as tall as me, her hair is longer, her nose (ha!) is bigger, and her hips (darn it all) are smaller. She was my fifth birthday present: We were born on the same day. She is my only sibling and she's the whole package: I love her to death *and* she drives me crazy.

Our personalities are opposite in one specific way: I am somewhat of an old soul and she is not. My sister is smart as a whip, compassionate, and deeply funny. She's also in no hurry to assume the trappings of adulthood (apart from her very successful career). But the last time Eliza visited me, she told me that she's thinking of getting a dog: a high-maintenance one, like a St. Bernard. She wants to settle down a little; she may even buy a house. But as much as I welcomed the news of my sister's impending adulthood, I couldn't help but have my doubts.

So when our birthday rolled around, I called a florist in the city where she lives. I had them tie a tag on a Meyer lemon tree. She called me on her way home from picking it up, the glossy-leafed lemon tree in her backseat.

"So . . ." she said.

"Well," I said. "Number one, you like to cook." "And number two, keep a tree alive and maybe you can get a dog."

Maybe in the spring she can make herself a lemon pound cake with homemade lemon extract. Thanks to her amazing big sister.

1 cup (2 sticks) unsalted butter, room temperature

3 cups sugar

5 eggs

1 (3-ounce) box lemon-flavored instant gelatin

1 tablespoon fresh lemon juice

1 teaspoon lemon extract

3 cups all-purpose flour

¼ teaspoon baking soda

¼ teaspoon salt

1 cup buttermilk

Preheat the oven to 350°F. Spray a Bundt pan (or four 4 × 7-inch loaf pans) with nonstick cooking spray.

In a large bowl, cream the butter and sugar. Add the eggs one at a time, and then add the gelatin, lemon juice, and lemon extract.

In a separate bowl, sift together the flour, baking soda, and salt. Alternately add the flour mixture and the buttermilk to the butter mixture and stir well. Pour the batter into the prepared pan.

Bake until a wooden toothpick inserted into the center of the cake comes out clean, 1 hour. Transfer to a wire rack and let cool for about 10 minutes before inverting onto a serving plate.

TEA CAKES

1 cup (2 sticks) unsalted butter, room temperature

1 cup sugar

2 eggs, beaten

1 teaspoon vanilla extract

3 cups all-purpose flour

2 teaspoons baking powder

Tea cakes seem to remind everybody of a certain old lady. These simple round cookies get grown men to speak longingly of their grandmothers.

For me, though, these cookies remind me of Miss Lela McMinn, who lives off Campground Road and is the voluntary grandmother to scores of children. She looks the part, too, with a cloud of snow-white hair and china-blue eyes.

Miss Lela runs a nice little cake business (and cupcakes, and tea cakes, and any baked good you might desire) out of her home. Well, not truly out of her home. The government mandates that any baked good (or processed good in general) that is sold must be produced in a commercial certified kitchen. This is a problem for folks wanting to run a bake-to-order business out of their homes: The fundamental definition of a commercial certified kitchen includes that it be a freestanding, nonresidential kitchen. When an inspector comes around and tells folks they need to build an entirely separate kitchen, most people throw in the towel.

Not Miss Lela. Instead, her now-deceased husband, Martin, built her one: a pleasant, airy space with scores of stainless-steel tables and over 200 cake molds. So Miss Lela bakes children's birthday cakes in every shape and size a child might imagine. Or, for that matter, grown men: She showed me the bikini mold with a wicked smile on her sweet face.

Themed cakes are nifty but don't get my heart pounding. It's Miss Lela's old-fashioned cakes make me swoon: round, three-layer classic cakes, standing tall and perfectly even, in flavors from coconut to caramel and many more.

During my time in the Deep South, I have found that the majority of sweet-faced, cheek-pinching, back-patting older women down here have backbones of pure steel. They have weathered vast losses and pains and have come through the storm shining and burnished. Miss Lela is no exception: She worked in a factory her adult life; she lost her husband too early; she lives with a son who is not all there owing to a birth injury. Yet she shines and continues to bake perfect cakes for not very much money, because it is not about the money; it is about what she chooses to do with her time, and baking cakes is one of Miss Lela's gifts to the world.

Or she did, anyhow. Miss Lela is going to the Lord fairly quickly now. Every time I hear a grown man mention his grandmother, see a tall shaggy coconut cake, or watch Cora place tea cakes into a shining cookie jar, I know I will think of her.

Preheat the oven to 350°F. Spray a baking sheet with nonstick cooking spray.

In a large bowl, cream the butter and sugar. Add the eggs and vanilla, and stir well.

In a separate bowl, combine the flour and baking powder. Add the flour mixture to the butter mixture and stir well. Using your hands, roll the batter into 2-inch balls and put them on the prepared baking sheet.

Bake until set and slightly golden on top, 10 to 12 minutes. Transfer to a wire rack and let cool completely.

Sweet AUTUMN CAKE

CAKE

2 pounds sweet potatoes, peeled and chopped into chunks

3 cups all-purpose flour

1 teaspoon baking soda

½ teaspoon baking powder

1 teaspoon ground nutmeg

1 teaspoon ground cinnamon

1 teaspoon ground allspice

1 teaspoon salt

1¾ cups (3½ sticks) unsalted butter, room temperature

2¾ cups granulated sugar

3 eggs

1 teaspoon vanilla extract

2 cups crushed graham crackers

1 cup chopped pecans

ICING

2 (8-ounce) packages cream cheese, room temperature

½ cup (1 stick) unsalted butter, room temperature

4 cups confectioners' sugar

1 teaspoon vanilla extract

CARAMEL

1 cup packed light brown sugar

½ cup half-and-half

¼ cup (½ stick) unsalted butter

¼ teaspoon vanilla extract

¼ cup crushed pecans, for garnish

SERVES 8 TO 10

Unlike the Steel Magnolia Cake (page 228), this cake has a serious wow factor. Cora sells it by special order during the holiday season, and our customers report that it is a crowd-pleaser. It is also insanely delicious: light, flavorful, sweet without being cloyingly sweet. I highly recommend it.

Preheat the oven to 350°F. Grease three 9-inch cake pans with butter.

For the cake, put the potatoes in a saucepan and cover with water. Set over medium-high heat, bring to boil, and cook until soft, 25 minutes. Drain, transfer to a stand mixer fitted with the paddle attachment, and beat until mashed. Let cool for 10 minutes or so.

In a medium bowl, sift together the flour, baking soda, baking powder, nutmeg, cinnamon, allspice, and salt.

In a stand mixer fitted with the whisk attachment, beat 1 cup of the butter and the granulated sugar. Add the eggs one at a time, beating well after each one. Add the vanilla. Add the dry ingredients to the butter mixture, alternating with the sweet potatoes.

In a large bowl, combine the graham cracker crumbs, pecans, and remaining ¾ cup (1½ sticks) butter. Press into the prepared cake pans. Divide the cake batter among the pans. Bake until a wooden toothpick inserted into the center of the cakes comes out clean, about 30 minutes. Transfer the pans to a wire rack and let cool for about 10 minutes. Turn the cakes out onto the wire racks and let cool completely.

For the icing, in a mixing medium bowl, beat the cream cheese, butter, confectioners' sugar, and vanilla until smooth.

For the caramel, in a skillet set over medium-low heat, combine the brown sugar, half-and-half, and butter. Cook, whisking, until thickened, about 10 minutes. Add the vanilla. Remove the pan from the heat and let cool completely.

Put 1 cake layer on a serving plate and frost the top with the icing.
Repeat with the second and third cake layers, and finish by frosting
the sides of the cake. Drizzle the cooled caramel over the top of the
cake, garnish with the crushed pecans, and serve.

CHOCOLATE BUTTERMILK *Cake*

CAKE

2 cups all-purpose flour

2 cups granulated sugar

¼ cup unsweetened cocoa powder

½ teaspoon salt

1½ teaspoons baking soda

½ cup buttermilk

½ cup vegetable oil

½ cup (1 stick) unsalted butter

2 eggs, lightly beaten

1 teaspoon vanilla extract

FROSTING

½ cup (1 stick) unsalted butter

⅓ cup unsweetened cocoa powder

1 tablespoon buttermilk

1 teaspoon vanilla extract

2 cups confectioners' sugar, sifted

3 tablespoons milk (as needed)

SERVES 8 TO 10

At this moment in time, Annaliese is at the store with me more often than Caspian. She has a modicum—the faintest, smallest dribble—of self-control, whereas Caspian wants the crackers! The cookies! The candy! A yogurt! A sparkle drink! All at the same time!

Barring the occasional kleptomaniac raid, Annaliese does pretty well. But we have set down some strict guidelines in the store because she knows the vast majority of our customers and has a tendency to barge into their meals. So one rule is that she is not allowed to sit with folks unless they specifically invite her.

The other day, I scolded her for sitting with Dr. Barry and Charmie Weeks, the dentist and his lovely assistant / office manager / wife.

Later, Mrs. Charmie said, "But, Alexe, I invited her." So I went and found my little girl hiding out between the orange and tomato carts, and I knelt down.

"I'm sorry, Annaliese," I said. "I didn't realize Mrs. Charmie asked you to sit with them."

She looked up and beamed. "That's okay, Mama," she said. "Everyone makes mistakes." And she skipped to the back of the store and scooted next to Mrs. Charmie.

A burden lifted off my shoulders. It's true. Everyone does make mistakes.

This chocolate buttermilk cake is pretty bombproof, however. I've yet to see it mess up.

Preheat the oven to 350°F. Grease an 11 x 13-inch baking dish.

For the cake, in a large bowl, combine the flour, granulated sugar, cocoa powder, and salt.

In a small bowl, stir the baking soda into the buttermilk until dissolved. Let it sit undisturbed until it has grown to 1 cup, about 2 minutes.

In a small saucepan set over medium-high heat, bring 1 cup of water, the oil, and butter to a boil. Pour the mixture into the flour mixture, and stir until creamy. Add the buttermilk mixture, and then add the eggs and vanilla. Stir well. Pour the batter into the prepared pan.

Bake until a wooden toothpick inserted into the center of the cake comes out clean, 20 to 30 minutes. Let cool for 5 minutes, but frost while still warm.

For the frosting, in a medium saucepan set over medium heat, melt the butter. Add the cocoa powder, stir well, and remove the pan from the heat. Add the buttermilk, vanilla, and confectioners' sugar. If the frosting is too thick, add milk a little at a time until the frosting is creamy.

While the cake and frosting are both still warm, frost the top of the cake.

LANE CAKE

Cora went on a kick a while back where she made a forgotten Southern classic every week. These cakes have names like black-eyed Susan cake, Minnihaha cake, and mahogany cake.

That phase came and went, but the Lane cake has stuck around. Lane cakes come from Alabama via the inspired Emma Rylander Lane of Clayton, who first published the recipe two years shy of the twentieth century. The cake also got a mention in *To Kill a Mockingbird*, when Scout observes that "Miss Maudie baked a Lane cake so loaded with shinny it made me tight."

A Lane cake is a pretty three-layer cake that often has some alcohol mixed into the batter and is decked in an ethereal whipped frosting. Cora puts dried cherries and pecans in her filling. As for the liquor, that's between you and your mixing bowl.

CAKE

1 cup (2 sticks) unsalted butter, room temperature

2 cups sugar

4 eggs

1 teaspoon vanilla extract

3 cups cake flour

1 tablespoon baking powder

Dash of salt

1 cup whole milk

FILLING

8 egg yolks, beaten

1 cup sugar

½ cup (1 stick) unsalted butter

1 cup sweetened dried coconut

1 cup chopped dried cherries

1 cup chopped pecans

½ cup chopped raisins

1 teaspoon bourbon or whiskey (or however much you want!)

7-MINUTE ICING

1½ cups sugar

¼ teaspoon cream of tartar

1½ teaspoons light corn syrup

2 egg whites

1 teaspoon vanilla extract

Preheat the oven to 350°F. Spray the sides of three 8-inch cake pans with nonstick cooking spray and line the bottoms with parchment paper.

For the cake, in a stand mixer fitted with the whisk attachment, beat the butter and sugar. Add the eggs one at a time, and then add the vanilla.

In a separate bowl, sift together the flour, baking powder, and salt. Add the flour mixture to the butter mixture, alternating with the milk, until incorporated. Divide the batter among the prepared cake pans.

Bake until a wooden toothpick inserted into the center of the cakes comes out clean, 15 to 20 minutes. Transfer to a wire rack and let cool completely.

For the filling, in a medium saucepan set over medium heat, combine the egg yolks, sugar, and butter. Cook, stirring constantly, until the mixture thickens, about 3 minutes. Remove the pan from the heat and add the coconut, dried cherries, pecans, raisins, and bourbon. Set aside to let cool.

For the icing, in the top of a double boiler, combine 5 tablespoons of water, the sugar, cream of tartar, corn syrup, and egg whites. Cook, beating constantly with an electric hand beater, until it is combined completely and to a spreading consistency, about 7 minutes. Remove the pan from the heat and add the vanilla. Continue beating with the hand mixer until the icing is thick enough to spread, about 2 minutes.

When the cake is cool, put 1 cake layer on a serving plate. Spread half of the filling over the cake, top with a second cake layer, and spread the remaining filling over the top. Add the third layer. Frost the sides and top of the cake with the icing.

STEEL MAGNOLIA CAKE

SERVES 8 TO 10

CAKE

2½ cups all-purpose flour

1¾ cups granulated sugar

1 teaspoon baking soda

1 (15-ounce) can fruit cocktail, drained

PRALINE TOPPING

½ cup packed light brown sugar

¼ cup (½ stick) unsalted butter

3 tablespoons whole milk

1 cup confectioners' sugar

1 teaspoon vanilla extract

1 cup chopped pecans (optional)

First and foremost, this cake is not a pretty cake. That's all right. Sometimes the good things in life are not pretty.

The B.T.C. has a wide spectrum of customers. There are folks who buy imported olive oil and handmade pasta and French jam and heirloom vegetables, and then there are the people who come in and ask for a dollar's worth of souse (also known as headcheese) to go along with a sleeve of crackers for their lunch. Ladies come in wearing big netted hats for church and want three slices of liver cheese, two tomatoes, and maybe a handful of okra, a couple of Georgia peaches, a small brown bag of raw peanuts for boiling.

I love watching these different sorts of people convene at Cora's table, hovering around each other, sleeves touching. Because this cake is fairly unattractive, Cora often sets out bite-size samples. The folks with the imported everything and the ladies in the hats and the men dressed in fishing gear are side by side getting a taste, and they'll end up talking to each other. Not much, but a look in the eyes, a "That sure is good." And then maybe they'll buy something off Cora's table and maybe they won't, but this cake gets them to that moment. And that makes me happy.

Preheat the oven to 350°F. Spray a 9 × 13-inch baking dish with nonstick cooking spray.

In a large bowl, combine the flour, granulated sugar, baking soda, and fruit. Pour the batter into the prepared pan.

Bake until a wooden toothpick inserted into the center of the cake comes out clean, 30 to 40 minutes. Let the cake cool completely in the pan, about 1 hour.

For the topping, in a medium saucepan set over medium-high heat, bring the brown sugar, butter, and milk to a boil while whisking constantly. Cook, while continuing to whisk, for about 1 minute. Remove the pan from the heat and stir in the confectioners' sugar, vanilla, and pecans (if desired). Spread over the top of the cake.

FIRST OF ALL, let's talk about guilt. I come from a long line of anxious people, and anxiety and guilt go hand in hand, so I know all about guilt. Real guilt, like when I've done something I absolutely regret, but also amorphous guilt—the kind that floats around in my life and attaches itself to whatever issue is on my mind at any time. Right now, in fact, I am beating myself up because yesterday evening, after the workweek was over, I realized I have fresh cranberries and a ton of limes in the store right now, and why haven't I filled spare glass jars with the combo like I saw in a magazine the other day? It would be pretty, though an extra effort, and too often I am too bogged down in invoice filing and bill paying and schedule making and produce restocking to go the extra mile to make the store gleam.

Oh, I am good at guilt.

Local food advocates lean heavily on guilt. As long as the item in question is local, freshly picked, preferably organic, direct from a small farmer, and/or gluten-free, I am supposed to be comfortable with paying three to six times the market rate.

I love fresh food. Heaps of colorful beautiful produce? Yes, please. However, price matters. Price matters a lot, unless you're a 1 percenter, in which case you're probably not reading this book. You're at Dean & DeLuca, buying tiny little glass bottles of imported juice for four dollars.

In my family, we've forgone cable, car payments, exotic vacations, nice shoes, eating out more than once a week, and toys of child and adult persuasions, but there is no way we will ever scrimp on food. Our house is regularly stocked with Billy Ray's glass-bottled milk, fresh bread, quarts of thick local honey, Bonne Maman jam, Brown Cow yogurt, B.T.C.'s Bold coffee from High Point Coffee Roasters, and whatever fresh vegetables we feel like cooking, with not much regard to price. We probably spend $120 to $200 per week on food—not bad for exclusively shopping at a small market with no regard to price, but then, we don't buy a lot of stuff in packages.

Anyhow, all this goes to say is, figure out what works for your life at this particular moment and let the rest go. I used to bake my own bread: Right now, it's not possible for me to do so. That's okay. I'd also like to take up keeping bees and establish a regular yoga practice, but I think I need to wait until my kids are in school and the store smoothes out. Those hobbies will keep. I tell myself all the time that I don't have to do everything I'm interested in all at the same time.

That being said, here are a few notes from my experience.

On Chickens

Let's start with America's newest craze: chickens.

I am a big fan.

To be clear: I am a person who does not care for infants (babies are cute in theory but mind-numbingly dull in practice), indoor pets (They shed! They pee! They drool! They're animals! I wish my husband would listen to me!), or high-maintenance anything, yet I adore my chickens. Right now I have five duds I got from a rich lady on Craigslist. These useless hens haven't laid an egg in two months, but I still adore them, even if I am planning to get some pedestrian but productive Red Stars from the Amish farmers as soon as I get a chance.

The only real challenge in keeping chickens is just that: keeping them. Kagan calls them meat popsicles for all the carnivores in your neck of the woods. From coyotes to dogs to raccoons to weasels, everything loves a chicken for dinner. Or more accurately, a four o'clock in the morning snack.

This is not a PETA-friendly tale, so be warned. We had just gotten chickens. Kagan had built a very cool chicken house out of the scraps in the backyard. He is a doer but at times just a little bit teeny-weeny slapdash, so he'd brushed off our collective parents' warnings about weasels and the like and left cracks galore around doors, in the eaves, and so on.

We woke up about twenty minutes to dawn to the sound of dying chickens. They do not go quietly: Our hens were squawking for help.

Kagan vaulted out of bed and grabbed a flashlight. He was in the henhouse before I was even out of bed, and he saw a raccoon on the perch of our henhouse, a chicken backing away in front of him. He grabbed a length of metal rebar. Cornered the raccoon and speared it, up through the roof of the mouth and into the brain. (It did die quickly.)

It was a little hard to go back to sleep after that. The next day, Kagan spent an hour stretching small-gauge chicken wire over the eaves and around the doors. Nothing ever successfully penetrated the henhouse again—assuming we remembered to lock it up at night.

So make sure your henhouse—which can be surprisingly small, since hens really only sleep in it and lay eggs occasionally during the day—is secure. We have a simple trapdoor we open in the morning and close at night. It's a chore, sure, but not much of one. The hens hop out and head back in during the twilight, where they fly clumsily up to their perch (any branch or long piece of wood will do) and remain during the dark.

Something I didn't know before having hens is that in the dark, you can pick up a chicken and move her wherever you like. Some people have hens so domesticated they submit to being carried around like a stuffed animal, but ours have never been cuddly. They go their way; we go ours. But once a hen has roosted, you can pick her up and she will be as compliant as you could wish. Useful if you are moving, like we just did.

In terms of actual care: We clean the chicken house once in a while, taking out soiled straw and replacing with fresh. We used to have a rooster (never ever have more than one—boys don't share well), and he was a smaller breed, so his crow wasn't ear-shattering, just pleasant. I liked having a rooster: He showed his ladies where food was with a special cluck and he alerted us if there was a neighborhood dog in the area. Unfortunately, he died, and our next rooster was big and mean, too hard on the ladies, so we ate him.

Butchering is a whole separate chapter, but honestly, skip it unless you're a hard-core farming type, in which case you don't really need my advice.

We collect eggs daily (or at least we used to). Once we had a problem with chicken mites, teeny little crawly bugs that we could see in the straw. But we started letting the chickens free-range a bit more so they had access to dust and dirt (hens love a dirt bath) and the problem solved itself. We give them clean water, regular chicken pellet feed we buy at the local feed store, and plenty of kitchen scraps. Feeling guilty about not wanting to have a compost pile? Hello, chickens! They especially adore my children's uneaten Cheerios and spaghetti strands, rotten melons and tomatoes from the B.T.C., and, weirdly, hard-boiled eggs. Though we don't make a lot of those these days (damn heritage chickens!).

I'd also like to add that if you're a gardener or a person who likes spending time outside in general, and you have a baby capable of sitting up but not yet moving, chickens rock. We'd just moved into what my family calls the blue house when Caspian was born in June, and by the fall, I was planting rosebushes and daffodil bulbs with abandon. Yet it was hard to find ways to keep him content for ten minutes or so at a stretch.

Voilà! Stale bread and chips crushed and spread three feet away from the baby! He adored watching the chickens peck and jostle, and I adored getting to sink my spade into the dirt while my baby was happy and getting some vitamin D.

One final note: Chickens are easier than dogs. If you can care for a dog, you can certainly have chickens. I am not sure why most people don't.

On Growing Food

I should know more about this than I do. After all, my mother had a vegetable garden; so did my grandfather. Unfortunately, they didn't make me help much with theirs, beyond the occasional June-bug picking/massacre. So when I set out to make my own garden, I had basically no idea what I was doing. Nor did I have any equipment. And Kagan is cheap and I hate equipment. (It never works right! Arg!)

So what I did was this: Buy a spade, check out a lot of library books, consider aesthetics—always important to me—and figure out what I was actually willing to do.

A public library is a beautiful thing, y'all.

The idea that really resonated with me was that of what the French call a *potager:* a kitchen garden, with a variety of fruits, vegetables, cutting flowers, and herbs, designed with aesthetics and seasonality in mind. Raised beds, a charming fence; a place to be rather than a place to work.

I am not sure my last two gardens ever fully lived up to my vision, but the one at the blue house got close: artfully laid out, a bed for strawberries, a redbud tree surrounded by Spanish bluebells and Thalia daffodils to keep me company in the early spring, various other beds full of herbs and vegetables, grass walks in between, a fence made out of bamboo.

That garden had successes (zinnias, sunflowers, cucumbers, the strawberry bed, herbs) and failures (winter squash, raspberries, snapdragons).

We laid it out like this: Kagan bolted together some big beams from some project or another in my desired shapes. I picked up a spade and spent a winter (remember, the frost line doesn't extend down very far here; elsewhere, I'd have to wait for spring) digging about eighteen inches deep. I'd create a trench in one place, dig up the root structure of the grass right next to it, flip the grass root side up into the trench, and move the new spot's dirt into the old spot's trench, so that the subsoil—the deep-down, generally not-so-great soil—was on the top of the bed and the good stuff was on the bottom.

This is a method called double digging, and I recommend John Seymour's *The Self-Sufficient Gardener* for a very good illustration that fixed the process clearly in my mind. It is labor-intensive, yes. I never did more than an hour at a time. It took a couple months at that slow pace. But the advantages are real: During last summer's drought, row-crop gardeners had to water daily to keep their plants from dying. I had to water once a week. Plus, you never do it again. One-time labor cost.

The theory works like this: Digging this deeply fluffs and aerates the soil, allowing roots to go deeper. You can thereby plant closer together and water less—pretty perfect for a kitchen garden, where space is confined. Also, leaving the weeds and the topsoil on the bottom of the hole means that those greedy little roots have a lovely surprise waiting for them when they get down there, causing plants to be healthier anyhow. I added manure in the fall, covered any bare beds with clover seed in the winter, and continued to build my soil that way.

I was only three years in when we moved up the street to our current home, but the soil got darker and richer and more crumbly every year. I never bought herbicides or fertilizer because I distrust chemicals and don't like spending money. It worked well for me. Things that didn't: an untreated bamboo fence, the aforesaid beams. We're doing the new garden with brick and metal and taking our time about it.

My biggest recommendation is to relax. Have fun! The cool thing about a garden is that you can always try again. There are no wrong answers, not really. The B.T.C. sells heirloom seeds from the Baker Creek Heirloom Seeds company (rareseeds.com), and I often watch folks pondering our seed selection, wondering if they should take a chance on growing scarlet okra or white eggplant or yellow tomatoes. It's cheap entertainment, y'all. A packet of seeds, even fancy ones like these, costs less than a latte at Starbucks. The correct choice is this: Buy the seeds. Plant them in some dirt. Water them once a week. See what happens.

On Sourcing

I don't live in a hub of localism. We visit Portland, Maine, Vermont, and Virginia pretty regularly in the course of seeing kinfolk, and those places rock. Good food from earnest people aboundeth.

Down here, it's a little different. At the B.T.C., we try to be transparent. If a food item is available locally *and*—and this is a big *and*—I think I can sell it, we try to carry it.

Sometimes people assume every banana, December tomato, and frozen vegetable we stock is locally grown. They are not. I have yet to find a Mississippi banana tree.

So we work with what we have: lots of local vegetables in the summer, fewer in the fall, practically none in the winter. Local milk, ice cream, eggs, grits, honey, bread, and coffee year-round. Maybe I shouldn't say this, this being a cookbook and all, but I hardly ever shop with a recipe list and hate it when customers come in clutching them because it closes their eyes to what's right there. We don't have figs every day, but when we do, they were picked that morning. To hell with what the *Ladies' Home Journal* says, now's the time to buy some figs! Same with kale and arugula and Brussels sprouts and asparagus. I earnestly recommend shopping in small stores, asking the grocer what is good that day, and going home with something beautiful, for which you can *then* find a recipe.

You're happier, your belly is happier, and your pocketbook is happier: in-season produce is generally prettier, tastier, and cheaper than the out-of-season alternatives.

That being said, my family buys bananas. We eat spinach and carrots—both cool-weather crops—year-round. But boy, springtime carrots straight out of the ground are a whole different animal. Make sure you try them.

While I'm preaching, let me get to hollering: Don't make assumptions, y'all.

One of my charming habits as a grocer is dragging my friends and family to grocery stores wherever I am on vacation. What can I say? It's my idea of a good time. And so I have pictures of myself holding quail eggs in front of the oldest grocery store in North America (Quebec City); posing with my sister in D.C. at Eastern Market; buying cheese at a creamery in New Orleans; loving on some raspberries at Rosemont Market in Portland (Maine); eating Popsicles outside of the co-op in Shrewsbury, Vermont.

Price-compare produce between Whole Foods and a small grocery store someday. Sure, the big store will have killer sales: things they are giving away to get you in the door. But pretty often, fresh food is cheaper, prettier, and more truly local at the small stores, especially those often-ethnic and completely awesome produce-only small markets. Man, I love those places. And then there's the Italian stores! With the guys behind meat slicers and wheels of cheese

and three rows of pasta and meatballs. I adore meatballs.

I've read at least eight articles suggesting that a sense of community makes you live longer, and more than six options—simply choices—of the same item stresses you out.

I earnestly believe this. I also know something else: Just by walking into those big stores, which feels like an occasion, where they are spraying scents in the air to titillate your appetite and playing music to quicken your pulse and spending calculated amounts of money on proven-to-work marketing strategies, you'll end up spending more anyhow.

We don't do any of that, because, one, it costs too much and, two, it takes too much time. If the B.T.C. smells like soup, it's because Dixie's making soup. If it smells like pie, Cora's probably baking. We play bluegrass mostly, because my customers like it and it makes the store seem happier. Also, it makes all my different kinds of customers comfortable. If I want something to get your attention, I set a bowl of it on the counter with a sign. Folks often buy more than what they came in for, but I hope they don't ever buy things they won't use.

I suppose big stores have their uses (eighteen different varieties of ketchup!), but I can tell you this: We live our life without them 98 percent of the time. And we're living well.

Shop small. Be happier. Live longer. Enough said.

Dixie's PICKLED EGGS

MAKES 3 DOZEN

The B.T.C. sells pickled okra, beets, beans, watermelon rind, dill pickles, bread and butter pickles, and sometimes asparagus, but I refuse to stock any pickled eggs other than Dixie's. These are fantastic with beer.

4 cups white vinegar

½ cup red wine vinegar

4 garlic cloves

1 cup sugar

¼ cup salt

¼ cup premixed pickling spices, such as McCormick

1 teaspoon crushed red pepper flakes

½ teaspoon ground cloves

1 cinnamon stick

1 bay leaf

1 large sprig fresh dill

3 dozen hard-boiled eggs, peeled

In a large pot set over medium-high heat, bring the vinegars, garlic, sugar, salt, pickling spices, pepper flakes, cloves, cinnamon stick, bay leaf, and dill to a boil, stirring to dissolve the salt and sugar. Turn off the heat and let cool to room temperature.

Put the eggs in a large container and cover with the brine. Refrigerate the eggs for at least 48 hours before serving. The eggs will keep in the brine in the fridge for 14 days.

Acknowledgments

Alexe

I would like to thank the town of Water Valley and the state of Mississippi for making my life wider and deeper than I ever knew it could be.

I thank my mother and father for all of their support throughout my life and in this wild-hearted endeavor.

I thank my agent, Sharon Bowers, for reaching out to me and summoning this book forward.

I thank our editor, Ashley Phillips, for her keen editorial comments, her help unloading bananas that autumn morning, and for believing in this book.

To the Clarkson Potter team: Pam Krauss, Doris Cooper, Rica Allannic, Marysarah Quinn, Sigi Nacson, Linnea Knollmueller, Erica Gelbard, Anna Mintz, and Carly Gorga.

Dixie, there is only one way in which you could be more perfect and you know what that is. Thank you for everything.

To Cora, for showing up and smiling, smiling, smiling.

To Lori, who came back after this book was written and whom we will never let leave again.

To the girls and boys of the B.T.C., keep the music playing and I love every one of you, sometimes. A huge thanks to my B.T.C.-ers, the people who walk through the door: you are why we're here. Unending thanks.

To Annaliese and Caspian, who lend me out and ride shotgun and talk folks into buying kiwis and crack the eggs for me.

And lastly, most importantly, to Kagan, who makes me believe all things are possible.

Dixie

To Alison Wilkes and Libby Furr for being the "moms" in my life and for supporting me, encouraging me, and believing in me.

To Alida Moore and Jaime Harker for all of your help and support. You represent everything a friend should be and more.

To Coulter Fussell for opening the doors to make this book possible.

To Danny Wayne Edwards for being a father figure and the only real cowboy I have ever known.

To all the people of Water Valley for welcoming me into your community and hearts with open arms.

To Alexe van Beuren for putting up with me on a daily basis, supporting me, encouraging me, trusting me, and sharing not only your business but your two amazing children with me. Together we move mountains, one apple at a time.

And finally to my grandmother Vetra Alderson Stephens for all the love and for teaching me the important things about life and love. Your life and legacy live on with me in the food I cook each day.

Index

Sunday Breakfast Special

#1: Blueberry Pancakes w/ side of sausage or bacon $5.99

#2: Toasted Croissant w/ Nutella + banana slices $3.99

Special

HOT

ROASTED TURKEY & MUENSTER on a toasted bagel w/ lettuce, tomato, & red onion cherry mayo $5.99

LUNCH SPECIAL

Smoked Turkey ***HOT***

on a croissant with provolone with cucumber·dill, lettuce, tomato, bread & pickles

BTC CHEF SALAD

with mixed greens, chedder & mont. jack cheese, ham, turkey, tomato cucumber, boiled egg, bacon

Choice of ranch, 1000 island or cucumber dill dressing. $7.99

SPECIAL SALAD

BASIL PARM SALAD CHICK with lettuce & tomato onion